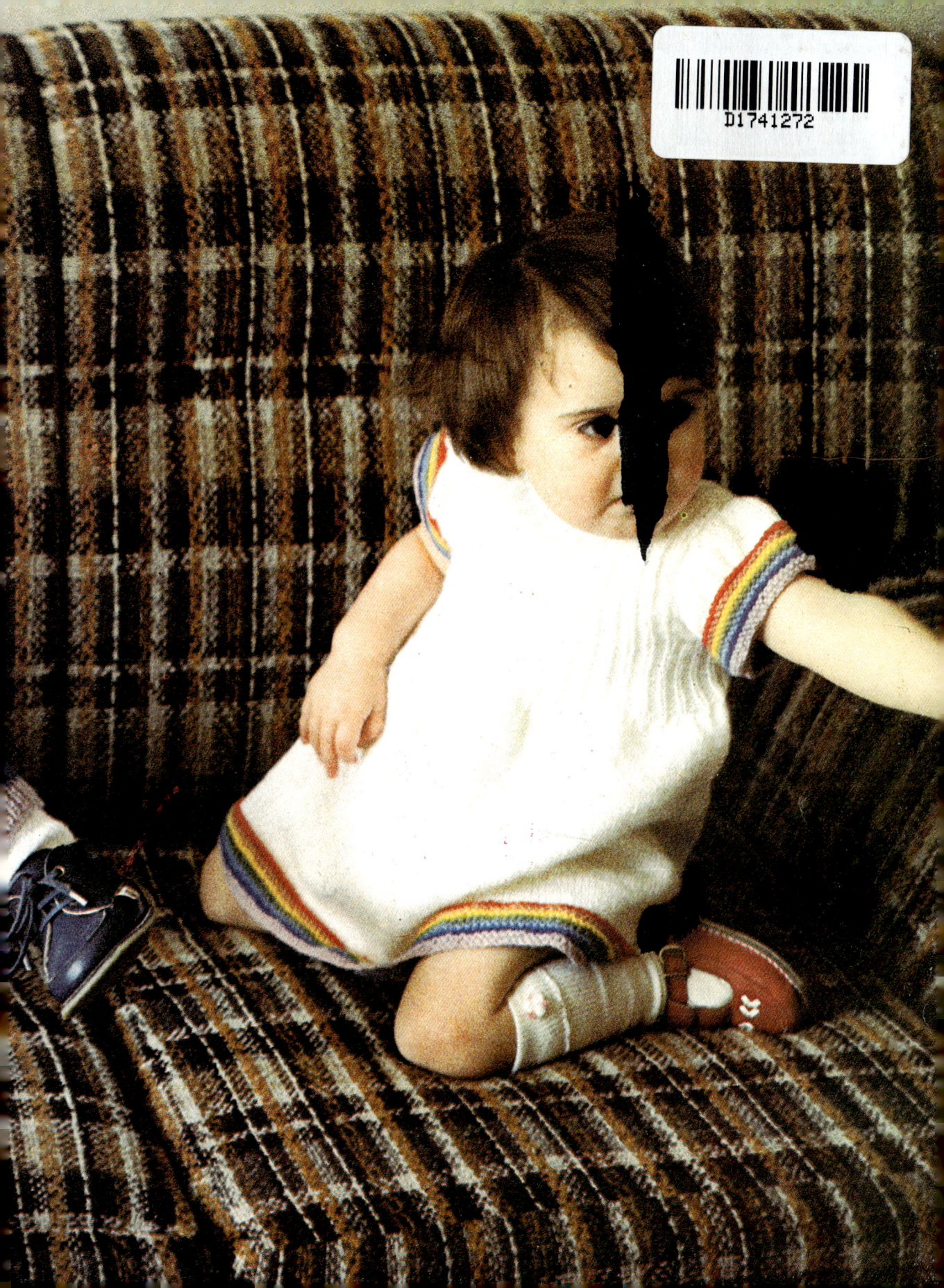

SUPERKNITS

JOY GAMMON

SUPERKNITS

PATTERNS FOR CHILDREN'S CLOTHES

W.H. ALLEN · LONDON
1985

For Children

Typeset by Phoenix Photosetting, Chatham
Printed and bound in Spain
for the Publishers W. H. Allen & Co. PLC
44 Hill Street, London W1X 8LB

ISBN 0 491 03521 7

Acknowledgements

The publisher and author would like to thank the following
for their help with this book:

Bob Enever and Simon Gardner for the photographs;
Les Gammon for the knitting charts;
Mothercare for the props used in the photographs
and for the additional clothes worn by the models;
Natalie Croft, Matthew, Lucy, Laurie and Jamie Erikson,
Joe and Emma Fitzgerald, Taryn and Cassie Gordon,
Ben Hart and Rebecca Walmsley for modelling the clothes;
and Mike Brett and Debbie Hart for designing the book.

CONTENTS

INTRODUCTION

Knitting has a long and complex history, bound up, or even knitted in, with surprising factors such as politics, royal patronage, employment statistics, wars and revolutions. The Tudors established it as an industry, and it has always had its place as a more humble fireside craft. People have knitted altar gloves for popes, and balaclavas for tommies at the front. Knitting has been part of a desperate struggle for subsistence and survival in crofting economies, as well as time-consuming nonsense for the well-to-do. It has even been used, because of its possible translation into numbers and letters, as a form of code. People do not suspect an innocent knitter of 'writing' messages, and this has served many a resistance worker well, ever since *les tricoteuses* at the guillotine. However, through all this exciting and chequered history, knitting has never been such fun! Fashion always repeats itself, but at the moment it seems to be repeating everything all at once, and anything (literally) goes.

Knitting is not difficult, and so anyone can be as zany as they like with it, and this, as well as all of the beautifully designed yarns to choose from, have made modern knitting a combination of lovely high fashion and over-the-top ideas, both of which are within reach of people's pockets and skills, and both of which knitters can use to whatever degree they wish.

Many people feel slightly inhibited about walking around wearing a dinosaur or a tree, but children have no such reservations, and, within the sizes covered by this book love to wear the unusual, the special and the unexpected.

So there are jumpers that do things, that squeak or jangle or have detachable bits to play with. There are horrid scarves to frighten people with, and toys to charm, dresses with surprise toys, surprise shapes or simply surprise colours. There are objects too: squashy cushions to love and sit on, and even to learn to tell the time with, as well as the essential assortment of teddies.

There is also a rainbow set for the very young, with both traditional and modern styles there to choose from. Perhaps gran could make the shawl, mum the christening gown, auntie the dungarees and elder brother the mittens. Even big sister would enjoy making one of the simple T-shirts.

Whichever of the patterns you choose to make, they are all practical, washable and extremely wearable, and I hope that all of you will find they give you endless pleasure and fun!

USEFUL INFORMATION

MATERIALS USED

On each pattern, the particular yarn used is specified, but there is no reason why other yarns that you have, or that you especially want to use, should not be substituted as long as you are very careful to work at the tension specified in the pattern chosen. Any scraps can be used for finger puppets, bits of patterning or colour and embroidery, of course.

I hope that throughout you will impose your own ideas on these basic patterns and use whatever colours you like, as well as altering characters and details into things that you prefer. If your children, for example, prefer cats to dogs, or hamsters to mice, then alter faces, features, ears and tails, so substituting chosen creatures.

The yarns that I used are specified in each pattern. In the event of any of the yarns being difficult to obtain, the following addresses will prove helpful:
Wendy Wools; Carter & Parker Ltd, Gordon Mills, Guiseley, West Yorkshire LS20 9PD; White Buffalo Mills Ltd, 545 Assinboine Avenue, Brandon, Manitoba 7272401, Canada; White Buffalo Mills Ltd, P.O. Box 506, Lynbrook, New York 11563, USA

Patons: Patons and Jaeger Ltd, Patons and Baldwin Ltd, P.O. Box, Darlington DL1 1YQ

Sirdar: Sirdar PLC, Flanshaw Lane, Alverthorpe, Wakefield, West Yorkshire WF2 9ND; Kendex Corporation, 31332 Via Colinas, 107 Westlake Village, California 91362, USA; Diamond Yarn (Canada) Corp., 153 Bridgeland, Unit 11, Toronto M6A 2Y6, Ontario, Canada

H. G. Twilleys Ltd, Roman Mill, Stamford, Lincolnshire PE9 1BG; also widely available in the USA.

GUIDE TO USING KNITTING CHARTS

Charts for the picture knitting are a stitch by stitch diagram of what colours to knit. The first and every alternate odd-numbered row will always be knitted and worked from right to left on the diagram, beginning your first contrasting coloured stitch as given in the particular pattern. The second and every alternate even-numbered row will always be purled and worked from left to right on the diagram. As you go along, you will be able to relate the coloured stitches in the row which you are working, to those in the previous row, and so watch the picture grow.

TENSION OR GAUGE

In almost all knitting patterns, including the ones in this book, you will see a reference to tension or gauge. This simply means the number of stitches and rows per inch which a particular piece of knitting achieves. This is of course governed by the size of each stitch.

If you do more knitting, and perhaps begin to design for yourself, you need to know how to measure tension because the size of the garment you are making – suppose it is meant to be 34 inches all round – will be dictated by the number of stitches and their size.

For example, if there are 6 stitches per inch, there will be 204 stitches all around your garment. But imagine what will happen if each of your stitches is a little bigger so that there are only 5 stitches per inch. If you still have 204 stitches, the distance round the garment will be

8

204 divided by 5, which is over 40 inches i.e. three sizes too big!

To get your tension correct, use the recommended needles and cast on enough stitches to give a width of about 5 inches at the recommended tension. Work in the stitch pattern suggested until you have a 5-inch square, and cast off loosely (or, if you are brave enough, simply slip the work off the needle and handle it carefully). Measure across the central 4 inches how many stitches per inch you have. Compare this with the recommended tension. Too many stitches per inch? Your stitches are too small. Change to needles one size larger and knit another square. Too few stitches per inch? Your stitches are too large. Change to needles one size smaller and knit another square. Continue doing this until your tension is the same as the recommended one, then knit your garment on needles which are the size you have chosen (because they suit the way you knit).

If other needle sizes are given in the pattern, for example, welts and ribbing are usually worked on needles two sizes smaller than those used for the main part, then you too should use needles two sizes smaller than the ones you have chosen to achieve the recommended tension.

MAKING UP

When you have knitted a garment, you will of course, unless you have been very clever, have several pieces of work which need fastening together. Here are a few points which might help. Very few yarns today need pressing, and it is better only to consider pressing wool yarns. If you do press, pin the garment piece out first, then press with a warm iron gently on a damp cloth.

When pinning knitting together, use the easily visible large coloured-headed pins, as dressmakers pins get lost in the yarn with potentially nasty consequences! Pin both ends first, then middle to middle, then the middles of each half, and so on. This matches the knitting evenly; otherwise, knitting is so stretchy that if you begin at one end and work towards the other, almost certainly, one piece will turn out longer than the other. Always check that you have matched any shapings or patterns that

should be matched, before you begin to sew.

Use the yarn with which you knitted to sew the garment up, so that it does not show, and so that it behaves and washes like the rest of the garment. The only exceptions to this are the very hairy or lumpy yarns which are horrible to sew with. For these, choose as near a match as you can in a similar smooth yarn. Sew the pieces together with a stitch that will stretch, like back stitch, and fasten on and off well at the beginning and end of a seam.

ABBREVIATIONS

alt.	=	alternate
approx.	=	approximately
beg.	=	beginning
cm	=	centimetre(s)
cont.	=	continue
dec.	=	decrease
foll.	=	following
gm	=	gram(s)
g.st.	=	garter stitch (i.e. every row K)
in	=	inch(es)
inc.	=	increase
K	=	knit
kg	=	kilogram(s)
m	=	metre(s)
mm	=	millimetre(s)
moss st.	=	moss stitch i.e. 1st row: K1P1, rep. to end. 2nd row: P1K1, rep. to end.
P	=	purl
psso	=	pass slip stitch over
rem.	=	remaining
rep.	=	repeat
rev.st.st	=	reverse side of stocking stitch
sl.	=	slip
st.	=	stitch
sts	=	stitches
st.st.	=	stocking stitch
tbl	=	through back of loop i.e. through the back of the stitch
tog.	=	together
togtbl	=	together through back of loop
yd	=	yard
yon	=	yarn over needle

AMERICAN AND BRITISH KNITTING TERMS

UK		US		UK		US
brackets	=	parentheses		work straight	=	work even
cast off	=	bind off		yarn over needle		
stocking stitch	=	stockinette stitch		yarn round needle	=	yarn over
swiss darning	=	duplicate stitch		yarn forward	=	bring yarn to front of work
(working a motif over knitted fabric)						
tension	=	gauge		yarn back	=	bring yarn to back of work

KNITTING NEEDLE SIZES

Original UK	000	00	0	1	2	3	4	5	6
Metric (mm)	9	8½	8	7½	7	6½	6	5½	5
USA	15	13	—	11	10½	10	9	8	7

Original UK	7	8	9	10	11	12	13	14
Metric (mm)	4½	4	3½ & 3¾	3¼	2¾ & 3	2½	2¼	2
USA	6	5	4	3	2	1	0	00

MICE

This cardigan has mice! They pop up all over the place, out of hole-shaped pockets, and I am not sure whether the holes were nibbled or the jumper is Emmental cheese. The jacket is a generous fit in a soft chunky yarn of which the rich yellow seemed most appropriate, although you could knit red Edam or Stilton blue if you preferred. (Picture p. 11)

Sizes
To fit chest 24(26 28 30)in, 61(66 71 76)cm.

Materials
In Wendy Shetland Chunky, 9(10 10 11) × 50gm balls of yellow yarn; 1(1 1 1) × 50gm ball of brown yarn. Scrap of black double knitting yarn and pink chunky yarn; small quantity of washable toy stuffing; 5 buttons

Tension
14 sts and 20 rows = 4in (10cm) on size ·3 (6½mm) needles in st.st.

TO KNIT BASIC CARDIGAN

Back
Using needles 2 sizes smaller than those chosen for main tension e.g. size 5 (5½mm), and yellow yarn, cast on 45(49 53 57) sts and work 2in (5cm) in K1P1 rib, beg. and ending each row K, and keeping rib correct in between. Inc. by 1 st. at each end of the last rib row. This gives a total of 47(51 55 59) sts.

Change to needles chosen for main tension e.g. size 3 (6½mm), and in st.st. work straight to a total length of 16½(17 19 20)in, 42(43 48 51)cm, ending with a P row.

Next row: cast off 16(18 19 21) sts and K to last 16(18 19 21) sts.

Place the centre 15(15 17 17) sts just worked on to a holder.
Cast off rem.sts.

Left front
Cast on 21(23 25 27) sts on smaller needles in yellow yarn and work 2in (5cm) in K1P1 rib as given for back. Inc. 1 st. at end only of last row on first and second sizes only: 22(24 25 27) sts.

Change to larger needles and st.st., beg. with a K row.
Work to a total measurement of 14½(15 16½ 17½)in, 37(38 42 44)cm, ending with a K row. *

To shape neck:
Next row: P2 and place these 2 sts on a pin. P to end.
**Dec. 1 st. at neck edge on the next 4 rows, then work straight until work measures the same as the back: 16½(17 19 20)in, 42(43 48 51)cm.
Cast off.

Right front
Work as given for left front as far as *.
Next row: P.

To shape neck:
Next row: K2 and place these 2 sts. on a holder, K to end.
Work as given for left front from **.

Sleeves
Make 2.
Using smaller needles and yellow yarn, cast on 25(25 27 27) sts.
Work 2in (5cm) in K1P1 rib as given for back.

Change to larger needles and work in st.st., inc.

1 st. at each end of every 5th row until there are
41(45 49 53) sts.
Work straight to a total length of
12½(13½ 15 16½)in, 32(34 38 42)cm.
Cast off loosely.

CHEESE HOLE POCKETS

Make 4, all alike.
Using larger needles and yellow yarn, cast on
6 sts.
Work 1 row in P.
Cont. in st.st. inc. 1 st. each end of every row to
12 sts.
Work 7 rows straight.

Dec. 1 st. each end of every row to 6 sts.
Work one row.
Cast off.

MICE

Make 4, all alike in brown yarn, in st.st.
Using larger needles, cast on 5 sts.
Next row: P.
Next row: K1, inc. 1 st. in each of the next 4 sts.
(9 sts).
Next row: P.
Next row: K, inc. 1 st. in every st. (18 sts).

Work 7 rows straight in st.st.
Next row: (K2tog., K5, K2togtbl) twice.
Next row: (P2togtbl, P3, P2tog.) twice.
Next row: (K2tog., K1, K2togtbl) twice.
Next row: (P2tog.) 3 times, run a thread
through these sts.

Ears
Make 8, all alike, in brown yarn in st.st.
Using larger needles, cast on 4 sts.
Work 4 rows straight.
Next row: dec. 1 st. each end.
Work 1 row.

Change to pink yarn.
Work 1 row.
Next row: inc. 1 st. each end.
Work 4 rows straight.
Cast off.

Tails
Make 1 for each mouse in pink yarn.
Using larger needles, cast on 10 sts.
Next row: K.
Next row: P.
Cast off.

BANDS

Right front
Up the complete right front edge, including welt
and ending at beg. of neck shaping, with right
side facing, pick up evenly, using yellow yarn
and smaller needles, and K51(53 57 61) sts, at
the rate of approx. 7 sts per 2in (5cm).
Work 6 rows in K1P1 rib.
Cast off in rib.

Left front
Pick up, in the same way as given for right front,
the same number of sts and K them.
Rib 3 rows, so ending at the neck edge.
Next row: rib 7(9 10 11) sts, [K2tog., yon, rib
11(11 12 13)] 3 times, K2tog., yon, rib to end.
Rib 2 more rows.
Cast off in rib.

Neckband
Carefully join both shoulder seams. With right
side facing, using smaller needles, pick up and
K4 sts across top of button band, 2 sts from pin,
8(8 10 10) sts up right neck slope,
15(15 17 17) sts from holder at back neck,
8(8 10 10) sts down left neck slope, 2 sts from
pin and 4 sts across top of buttonhole band:
43(43 49 49) sts.
Work 3 rows in K1P1 rib in the same way as
given for back.
Next row: rib to last 5, K2tog., yon, rib 3.
Work 2 more rows in rib.
Cast off in rib.

Making up
Do not press. Make up jumper with
6(6½ 7 7½)in, 15(17 18 19)cm deep armholes.
Attach cheese hole pockets, leaving about a
third of their edge unattached.
Seam and stuff the mice. Fold and attach the
ears, attach the tails, embroider eyes, noses and
whiskers.
Sew on buttons to match button holes.

"TYGER, TYGER"

This jumper is as much fun for the maker as for the wearer, because it can have as many leaves, trees, tigers and fruit as you like. You can also add snakes, macaws, flowers, beetles or anything you fancy. Unless you can be bothered to take them off every time, remember to make all the added bits washable. (Picture opposite)

Sizes
To fit chest 24–26(28–30)in, 61–66(71–76)cm.

Materials
In Sirdar County Style double knitting: 3(4) × 50gm balls of dark green yarn; 1(1) × 50gm ball of dark brown yarn. Small quantity of 3 different light greens; yellow and white yarns. Small quantity of washable stuffing. 2 bright beads. Fruit and leaf beads.

Tension
24 sts and 32 rows = 4in (10cm) on size 8 (4mm) needles in st.st.

TO KNIT BASIC JUMPER

Front and back
Both alike.
Using needles 2 sizes smaller than those chosen for main tension, e.g. size 10 (3¼mm), and dark brown yarn, cast on 85(97) sts.

1st row: (K1,P1) rep. to last st., K1.
2nd row: K1,(K1,P1) rep. to last 2 sts, K2.
Rep. these 2 rows until 2in (5cm) of rib have been worked.

Change to needles chosen for main tension, e.g. size 8 (4mm), and st.st.
Work a further 2in (5cm).

Change to dark green yarn.

Work straight to a total length of 15½(18)in, 39(46)cm.
Work 1(1½)in, 2½(4)cm in K1P1 rib.
Cast off in rib.

Sleeves
Both alike.
Using smaller needles and dark brown yarn, cast on 43(45) sts.
Work 2in (5cm) in K1P1 rib as given for back.
Change to larger needles and st.st.

Inc. 1 st. at each end of the 7th and every foll. 7th(8th) row until there are 63(69) sts; at the same time, after 2in (5cm) of st.st., change to dark green yarn.
Work straight to a total measurement of 13½(16½)in, 34(42)cm or required length to underarm.
Cast off.

Making up
Do not press. Join shoulder seams leaving 8(9)in, 20(23)cm neck opening.
Mark armhole depth at each side of the back and front to a depth of 7(7½)in, 18(19)cm.
Seam sides up to this point, matching colours.
Seam and insert sleeves.

TREES

Make 3, all alike in pale brown yarn, working throughout in st.st. on main size needles.
Cast on 72(75) sts.
Next row: K.
Next row: P.
Next row: K.
Next row: cast off 24 sts, P to end.
Next row: K.
Next row: cast on 24 sts at beg., P these sts, P to end.

Next row: K.
Next row: cast off 48 sts, P to end.
Next row: K.
Next row: cast on 48 sts at beg., P these sts, P to end.
Next row: K.
Next row: cast off 36 sts, P to end.
Next row: K.
Next row: cast on 48 sts at beg., P these sts, P to end.
Next row: K.
Next row: P.
Cast off.

LEAVES

Make 4 in each of the 3 light green yarns, i.e. 12 in all.
Using main size needles, cast on 18 sts.
Work in st.st. throughout.
Next row: K.

1st row: inc. 1 st. each end of row, in P.
2nd row: inc. 1 st. at end only of row, in K.
Rep. these 2 rows 3 more times (30 sts).

Next row: K to form centre rib.
1st row: dec. 1 st. at end only of row, in K.
2nd row: dec. 1 st. each end of row, in P.
Rep. these 2 rows 3 more times (18 sts).

Next row: K.
Cast off.

TIGER

Body
Using main size needles and yellow yarn, cast on 10 sts. Work in st.st. throughout.
Inc. 1 st. each end of next 4 rows (18 sts).

*Change to dark brown yarn.
Work 2 rows.
Change to yellow yarn.
Work 4 rows*.
Repeat from * to * 4 more times.

Work 2 rows in dark brown yarn.
Change to yellow yarn.
Dec. 1 st. each end of next 4 rows (10 sts).
Cast off.

Head
To make bottom half:
Using yellow yarn, cast on 5 sts.
Keeping right-hand edge of work straight throughout, inc. 1 st. at left-hand edge of every row 4 times (9 sts), working in st.st.
Work 14 rows straight.
Dec. 1 st. at left-hand edge of every row 4 times (5 sts).
Cast off.

To make top half:
Using yellow yarn cast on 5 sts.
Work throughout as given for bottom half but alternate yellow and brown yarns every 2 rows, ending with a yellow stripe.
Cast off in yellow.

Legs
Make 2, both alike.
Work throughout in alt. 2 row stripes of yellow and dark brown yarns.
Cast on 8 sts in yellow yarn and work 1½in (4cm) straight, in stripes, ending with a P row.
Next row: (K2tog.) rep. to end.
Run a thread through rem. sts.

Ears
Make 2, both alike.
Cast on 8 sts in yellow yarn and work 4 rows.
Dec. 1 st. each end of next 2 rows.
Inc. 1 st. each end of next 2 rows.
Work 4 rows.
Cast off.

Tail
Make 1.
Cast on 8 sts in yellow and work in 2 row stripes in st.st. as given for legs to a measurement of 4in (10cm) ending with a P row.
Next row: (K2tog.), rep. to end.
Run a thread through rem. sts.

Making up
Arrange the tree trunks and the tiger as you wish, then stitch on the pieces with a small amount of stuffing. Stitch on leaves, attaching them firmly, but as little as possible, so that they hang. Embroider the tiger's features and fold the ears in half and attach. Stitch on bead eyes, fruit, leaves or any other beads as desired.

TEDDY

Why shouldn't children's jumpers make a noise? Their owners do! This simple to knit teddy (see chart on p. 20), in a thick, warm chunky yarn, has a squeaker in his tum, and so answers back when squoken to. If you have difficulty getting squeakers, then the jumper works quite happily without, or teddy could have a little bell around his neck. Make sure the squeaker is easily removed for washing, or the bear will catch rather soggy laryngitis. (Picture p. 18)

Sizes
To fit chest 24(26 28 30)in, 61(66 71 76)cm.

Materials
In Sirdar Leisure-time chunky: 6(7 7 8) × 50gm balls of white yarn; 1(1 1 1) × 50gm ball of brown yarn. Scraps of black double knitting yarn. 1 toy squeaker.

Tension
14 sts and 18 rows = 4in (10cm) on size 3 (6½mm) needles in st.st.

Back
Using needles two sizes smaller than those chosen for main tension, e.g. size 5 (5½mm), cast on 47(49 53 57) sts.

1st row: (K1,P1) rep. to last st., K1.
2nd row: K1,(K1,P1) rep. to last 2 sts, K2.
Rep. these 2 rows until 2in (5cm) have been worked.

Change to needles chosen for main tension, e.g. size 3 (6½mm), and st.st.
Starting with a K row, work straight until work measures 10½(11 11½ 13)in, 27(28 29 33)cm, or required length to armhole, ending with a P row.

To shape armholes:
Cast off 2(2 2 3) sts at beg. of next 2 rows. * Dec. 1 st. at each end of next 3 rows.

For 3rd and 4th sizes only:
Next row: Dec. 1(1) st. each end of row.

For all sizes:
37(39 41 43) sts rem.
Work straight until armholes measure 5(5½ 6 6½)in, 13(14 15 16)cm, ending with a P row.

To shape shoulders:
Cast off 6(6 6 7) sts at beg. of next 2 rows, then 5(6 6 6) sts at beg. of foll. 2 rows.
Slip rem. 15(15 17 17) sts on to a holder for neckband.

Front
Work as given for back as far as *, working the bear from the chart on p. 20.
Dec. 1 st. at each end of next 3 rows.

For 3rd and 4th sizes only:
Dec. 1 st. at each end of the foll. 1(1) alt. rows.

For all sizes:
37(39 41 43) sts rem.
Work straight until front is 9(9 11 11) rows shorter than back to start of shoulder shaping, thus ending with a K row.

To shape neck:
Next row: P14(15 16 17) sts, turn and complete this side first.
** Dec. 1 st. at neck edge on next 3 rows.

For 3rd and 4th sizes only:
Dec. 1 st. at neck edge on following alt. row.

17

For all sizes:
11(12 12 13) sts rem.
Work 6 rows straight (work 1 row less here for 2nd side), thus ending at armhole edge.

To shape shoulders:
Cast off 6(6 6 7) sts at beg. of next row.
Work 1 row.
Cast off rem. 5(6 6 6) sts.
Slip next 9(9 9 9) sts at centre on to a holder for neckband.

With wrong side of work facing, rejoin yarn to neck edge of rem. sts and P to end.
Complete as given for first side from ** to end, reversing all shaping by working 1 row less where indicated.

Sleeves
Both alike.
Using smaller needles, cast on 25(27 27 29) sts.
Work 2in (5cm) in K1P1 rib as given for back.

Change to larger needles.
Work 4 rows in st.st., starting K.
Inc. 1 st. each end of next and every foll. 7th(8th 8th 8th) row until there are 35(37 39 41) sts.
Work straight until sleeve measures 11(13 13½ 14)in, 28(33 34 35)cm, or required length to underarm, ending with a P row.

To shape top:
Cast off 2(2 2 3) sts at beg. of next 2 rows.
Dec. 1 st. at each end of next 3(3 3 3) rows.
Dec. 1 st. at each end on every alt. row until 21(21 21 21) sts rem.
Dec. 1 st. at each end of next 3 rows: 15(15 15 15) sts.

Cast off 4(4 4 4) sts at beg. of foll. 2 rows.
Cast off rem. 7 sts.

Making up and neckband
Join left shoulder seam. Using smaller needles and with right side facing, K across sts on holder at back neck, dec. 1 st. at centre; pick up and K11(11 13 13) sts down left front slope; K across sts on holder at front neck; pick up and K11(11 13 13) sts up right front slope.
Work 4½(5½ 5½ 6½)in, 11(14 14 16)cm, in K1P1 rib as given for back.
Cast off loosely in rib.
Join right shoulder seam. Join side and sleeve seams. Insert sleeves. Do not press.

SQUEAKER POCKET

This pocket accommodates a squeaker up to about 2in (5cm) across; for larger squeakers add more sts.

Using needles chosen for main tension and brown yarn, work in st.st. throughout.
Cast on 6 sts.
Work 1 row.
Next row: inc. 1 st. each end of row.
Work 2in (5cm) straight in st.st.
Next row: Dec. 1 st. each end of row.
Cast off.

Making up
Slip st. pocket behind bear's tummy and insert squeaker.
You may prefer to loosely slip st. the pocket closed between removals of squeaker for each wash to prevent it getting lost or played with at inconvenient times!

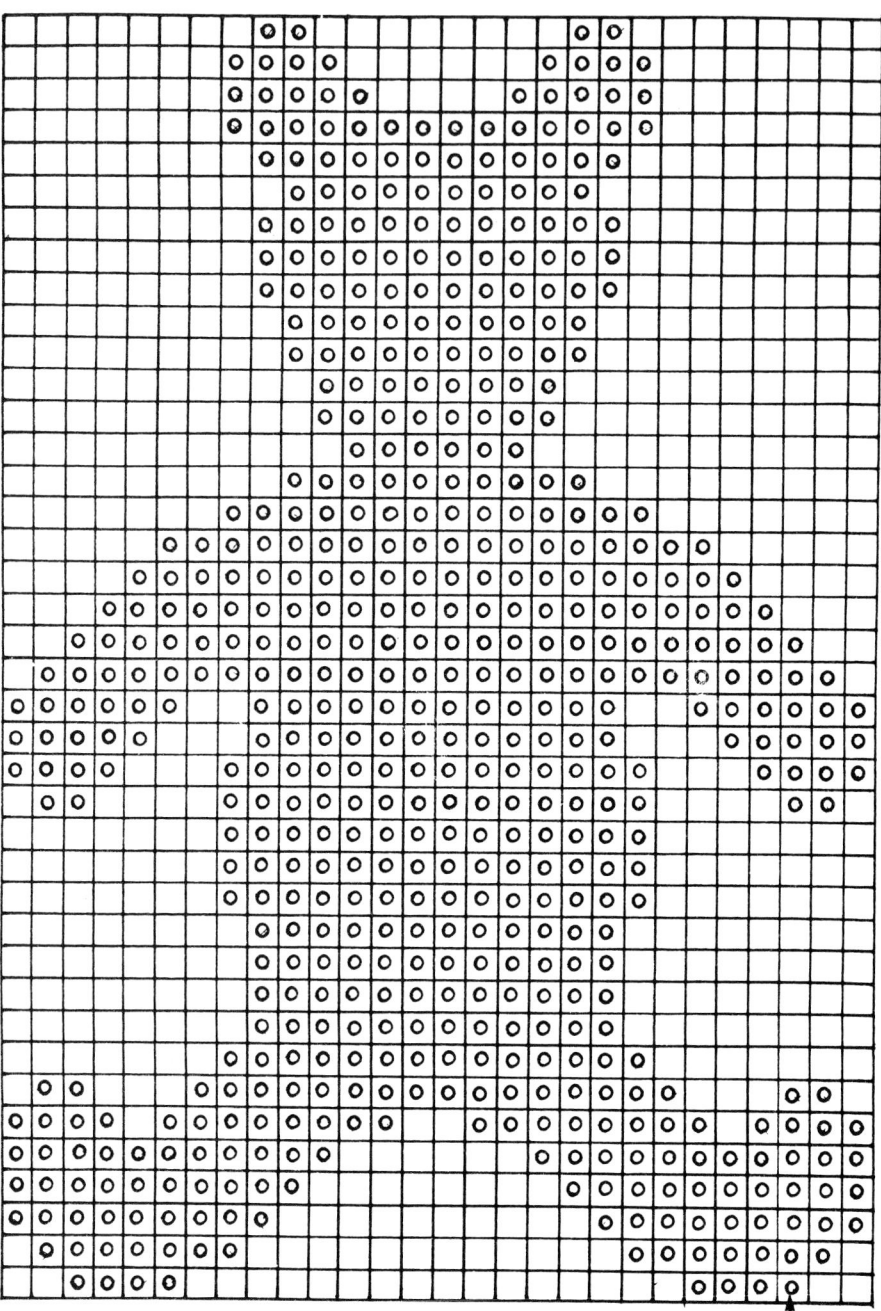

Begin brown yarn with this
st. as the 12th (13th, 15th, 17th,)
st. of the 5th (7th, 9th, 15th,)
row of st. st.

O   brown yarn
     All rem squares white yarn

CLOWN

Clowns have always been noisy, so this jumper jingles like a Morris Dancer and, as well as picturing a clown, has the traditional stripey red and yellow sleeves. It should really be worn with enormously baggy patched trousers and shoes 23 sizes too big! (Picture p. 23)

Sizes
To fit chest 24(26 28 30)in, 61(66 71 76)cm.

Materials
In Wendy Family Choice double knitting: 3(4 4 5) × 50gm balls of red yarn; 2(2 3 3) × 50gm balls of yellow yarn. Scraps of black and white double knitting yarns. 6 jingle bells. A very small quantity of washable toy stuffing.

Tension
24 sts and 32 rows = 4in (10cm) on size 8 (4mm) needles in st.st.

TO KNIT BASIC JUMPER

Back
Using needles 2 sizes smaller than those chosen for main tension, e.g. size 10 (3¼mm), and yellow yarn, cast on 79(83 89 95) sts.
1st row: (K1,P1) rep. to last st., K1.
2nd row: K1,(K1,P1) rep. to last 2 sts, K2.
Rep. these 2 rows until 18(20 20 20) rows have been worked.

Change to needles chosen for main tension, e.g. size 8 (4mm), and red yarn and work in st.st. throughout.
Work straight until work measures 10½(10½ 12 12½)in, 27(27 30 32)cm, or required length to underarm, ending with a P row.

To shape armholes:
Cast off 3(3 3 3) sts at beg. of next 2 rows.
Dec. 1 st. at each end of next 3(3 3 5) rows, then every alt. row until 61(65 69 71) sts rem. *
Work straight until armholes measure 5½(6 6½ 7)in, 14(15 16½ 18)cm, ending with a P row.

To shape shoulders:
Cast off 6(7 7 7) sts at beg. of next 4(4 4 4) rows, then 7(6 7 7) sts at beg. of the foll. 2 rows.
Slip rem. 23(25 27 29) sts on to a holder.

Front
Work as given for back as far as *.
Work straight until armholes measure 3½(4 4 4½)in, 9(10 10 11)cm.

To shape neck:
Work 24(25 26 26) sts, turn and complete this side first.
Dec. 1 st. at neck edge on next 3 rows, then every alt. row until 19(20 21 21) sts rem.
Work straight until armholes match those on the back, ending at outside armhole edge.

To shape shoulders:
Cast off 6(7 7 7) sts at beg. of next and every alt. row until 7(6 7 7) sts rem.
Work 1 row.
Cast off rem. sts.
Slip centre 13(15 17 19) sts on to a holder.
Work other side to match the first.

Sleeves
Make 2 both alike.
Using smaller needles and red yarn, cast on 43(43 45 45) sts.
Work 18(20 20 20) rows in K1P1 rib as given for back.

21

Change to larger needles and st.st.
Work the foll. stripe pattern throughout the rem. of the sleeve: 4 rows yellow, 4 rows red. At the same time, inc. 1 st. each end of the 7th and every foll. 9th(7th 8th 8th) row until there are 59(63 65 69) sts.
Work straight in stripes until sleeve measures 12½(13½ 15 16½)in, 32(34 38 42)cm, or required length to underarm, ending with a P row.

To shape top:
Cast off 3(3 3 3) sts at beg. of the next 2 rows.
Dec. 1 st. at each end of the next 5(5 5 5) rows, then every alt. row until 31(33 33 33) sts rem.
Dec. 1 st. each end of the next 5 rows.
Cast off 5(6 6 6) sts at beg. of the foll. 2 rows.
Cast off rem. sts.

Neckband
Do not press.
Join left shoulder seam. Using smaller needles and yellow yarn, and with right side facing, pick up and K sts across holder at back neck, working 2tog. at centre; 19(19 21 21) sts down left front slope; sts from front holder; and 19(19 21 21) sts up right front slope.
Work 2(2½ 2½ 2½)in, 5(6 6 6)cm in K1P1 rib as given for back welt.
Cast off very loosely in rib.

CLOWN'S FACE
Using needles chosen for main tension and white yarn, cast on 12 sts, work in st.st.
Inc. 1 st. each end of every row to 24 sts, then each end of every alt. row to 36 sts.
Work 12 rows straight.
Dec. 1 st. each end of every alt. row to 24 sts, then each end of every row to 12 sts.
Cast off, leaving long thread for making up.

Neck frill
Using needles chosen for main tension and yellow yarn, work in garter st. (all K).
Cast on 24 sts.
Next row: K.
Next row: inc. 1 st. in every st. (48 sts).
Work 3 rows straight.
Next row: *K8, turn, and, working on these sts, dec. 1 st. each end of every 4th row until there are 2 sts.
Work 1 row.
Next row: K2tog., fasten off*.
Rejoin yarn and rep. from * to * 5 more times.

Making up
Join all rem. seams. Attach clown's lightly stuffed face centrally on jumper front. Embroider eyes and mouth in black and red yarns and add a 1in (2½cm) black pompom nose. Embroider fringe of hair in yellow yarn. Attach neck frill, adding a bell to each point.

APPLES

This simple cardigan is decorated with an apple motif (see chart opposite). You can make it in bright colours or pale ones. You could add any other picture you like, as well as zany buttons. The basic pattern is an ideal one to use again in different ways. (Picture p. 27)

Sizes
To fit chest 24(26 28 30)in, 61(66 71 76)cm.

Materials
In Patons Beehive 4 ply: 3(3 4 4) × 50gm balls of pink yarn; 1(1 1 1) × 50gm ball of green yarn. 5 buttons.

Tension
28 sts and 36 rows = 4in (10cm) using size 10 (3¼mm) needles in st.st.

Back
Using needles 2 sizes smaller than those chosen for main tension, e.g. size 12 (2¾mm), and pink yarn, cast on 91(99 105 113) sts.
1st row: *K1,P1, rep. from * to last st., K1.
2nd row: **P1,K1, rep. from ** to last st., P1.
These two rows form the K1P1 rib.
Work 16 rows in rib, inc. 1 st. at end of the last row on 1st and 3rd sizes only: 92(99 106 113) sts.

Change to larger needles , e.g. size 10 (3¼mm), and st.st.
Working in pink yarn, follow the chart for the apples as given opposite; beg. the first green yarn st. as the st. marked (this is the 11th[14th 18th 10th] st. of the 5th st.st. row). Then cont. in pink yarn until work measures 9(10 11 12)in, 23(25 28 31)cm, ending with a P row.

To shape armholes:
Cast off 4 sts at beg. of next 2 rows.

1st row: K1, sl.1, K1, psso, K to last 3 sts, K2tog., K1.
2nd row: P.
Rep. last 2 rows until 32(35 38 41) sts rem.
Cast off.

Left front
Using smaller needles and pink yarn, cast on 41(45 49 51) sts.
Work 16 rows in rib as given for back welt, inc. 1 st. at end of last row on 1st and 4th sizes only: 42(45 49 52) sts.

Change to larger needles.
Work pattern from chart, beg. with marked st., which is the 8th(8th 12th 15th) st. of the 5th st.st. row.
Then cont. in st.st. until work measures the same as the back to armhole shaping, ending with a P row**.

To shape armhole and front edge:
Cast off 4 sts at beg. of row.
Next row: P.
1st row: K1, sl.1, K1, psso, K to last 3 sts, K2tog., K1.
2nd row: P.
3rd row: K1, sl.1, K1, psso, K to end.
4th row: P.
*** Rep these 4 rows, dec. 1 st. at armhole edge on every alt. row and at front edge on every 4th row until 24(24 16 16) sts rem.
Cont. to dec. at armhole edge as before, but dec. at neck edge on every 6th row until 4 sts rem.
Dec. at raglan edge only until 2 sts rem.
Next row: P2tog. Fasten off.

Right front
Work as given for left front as far as **, but for right front beg. working from the chart with the

marked st. that is the 8th(11th 11th 11th) st. of the 5th st.st. row, ending with a K row.

To shape armhole and front edge:
Cast off 4 sts at beg. of row.
1st row: K1, sl.1, K1, psso, K to last 3 sts, K2tog., K1.
2nd row: P.
3rd row: K to last 3 sts, K2tog., K1.
4th row: P.
Cont. as given for left front from *** to end.

Sleeves
Make 2.
Using smaller needles and pink yarn, cast on 39(41 45 57) sts.
Work 16 rows in rib as given for the back welt, inc. 4(2 5 3) sts evenly on last row: 43(43 50 60) sts.

Change to larger needles and st.st.
Work the chart as given, beg. with the marked st. that is the 10th(10th 13th 13th) st. of the 5th st.st. row; at the same time inc. 1 st. each end of every 4th row until there are 71(75 80 84) sts. Cont. without further shaping until work measures 11(12½ 14 15½)in, 28(32 36 39)cm, or required length, ending with a P row.

To shape top:
Cast off 4 sts at beg. of next 2 rows.
1st row: K1, sl.1, K1, psso, K to last 3 sts, K2tog., K1.
2nd row: P.
Rep. the last two rows until 11(11 12 12) sts rem.
Cast off.

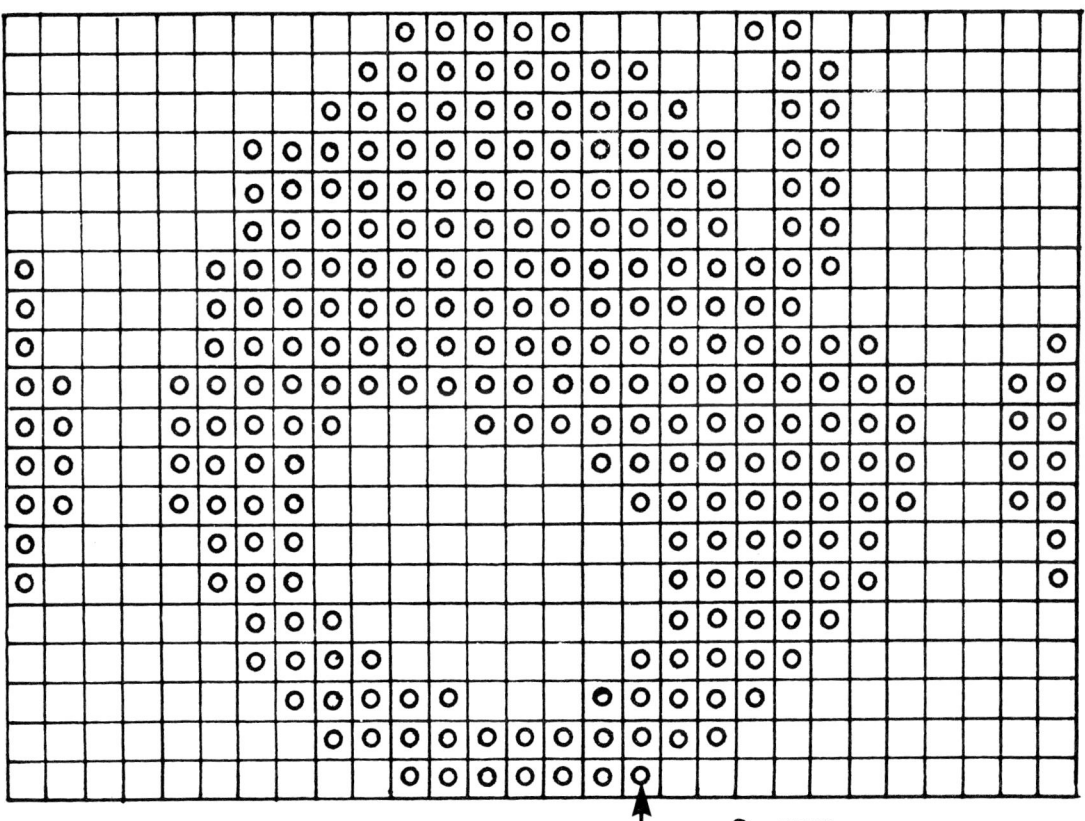

O green
All rem. sts = pink

Right front band

Sew the raglan seams.

Using smaller needles and pink yarn, and with right side facing, pick up and K62(69 76 83) sts to first neck shaping, 46(50 56 60) sts to top of front, 9(9 10 10) sts across sleeve top, and finally 16(17 19 20) sts to centre back of neck: 133(145 161 173) sts.

Work 6 rows in K1P1 rib as given for back welt, starting with a 2nd row.

To make buttonholes:

Next row: with wrong side facing, rib 74(78 89 91), * cast off 3 sts, rib 10(12 10 12) sts, (include st. on right-hand needle), rep. from * 3(3 4 4) times more, cast off 3, rib 4.

Next row: work in rib, casting on 3 sts over cast-off sts of previous row.

Work 6 rows in rib.

Cast off in rib.

Left front band

Work as given for right front band, picking up sts from centre back of neck and omitting buttonholes.

Making up

Make up all rem. seams. Sew on buttons to match buttonholes.

CHESS

These jumpers are especially for chess addicts, but they don't have to be worn with glasses and a frown! Anyone who likes an easy chequered jumper will enjoy them, and, if your children prefer, work the basic pattern alternating squares in the colours of other games and add different motifs. How about cream and brown yarns with snakes and ladders, or Scrabble with words? Swiss darning is such an easy way to embroider, that you can do any motifs you like. (See chart opposite for chess piece motifs.)

Sizes
To fit chest up to 26(up to 30)in, up to 61(up to 76)cm.

Materials
For the jumper, in Wendy Family Choice double knitting: 2(2) × 50gm balls of black yarn. 4(5) × 50gm balls of white yarn. Small quantity of grey yarns. For the slipover, in Wendy Family Choice double knitting 2(2) × 50gm balls of black yarn; 2(2) × 50gm balls of white yarn. Small quantity of grey yarns.

Tension
24 sts and 32 rows = 4in (10cm) on size 8 (4mm) needles in st.st.

TO KNIT BASIC JUMPER

Back
Using needles 2 sizes smaller than those chosen for main tension, e.g. size 10 (3¼mm), and white yarn, cast on 83(95) sts.
1st row: (K1,P1) rep. to last st., K1.
2nd row: K1,(K1,P1), rep. to last 2 sts, K2.
Rep. these 2 rows until 2in (5cm) have been worked, inc. 1 st. at end of last row: 84(96) sts.

Change to larger needles e.g. size 8 (4mm) and st.st.

*For smaller size only:
1st row: 12 sts black (12 sts white, 12 sts black) rep. to end.
NB On the smaller size, on one half of the garment, the colours can be reversed, so keeping pattern correct up the side seam.

For larger size only:
1st row: (12 sts white, 12 sts black) rep. to end.

For all sizes:
Work 2nd to 16th rows so that the stitches are worked in the same colour as they were in the 1st row.

For smaller size only:
17th row: 12 sts white (12 sts black, 12 sts white) rep. to end.

For larger size only:
17th row: (12 sts black, 12 sts white) rep. to end.

For all sizes:
Work 18th to 32nd rows so that the stitches are worked in the same colour as they were in the 17th row*.
Rep. these 32 rows of chequered pattern, from * to *, throughout.
Cont. until work measures 10(12)in, 25(30)cm, ending with the 31st (15th) row of pattern.

To shape armholes:
Keeping chequered pattern correct, cast off 12(12) sts at beg. of row, work to last 12(12), cast off these 12 sts**.
Work 3(4) lines of complete squares on these rem. 60(72) sts, but end with 15th row of check.

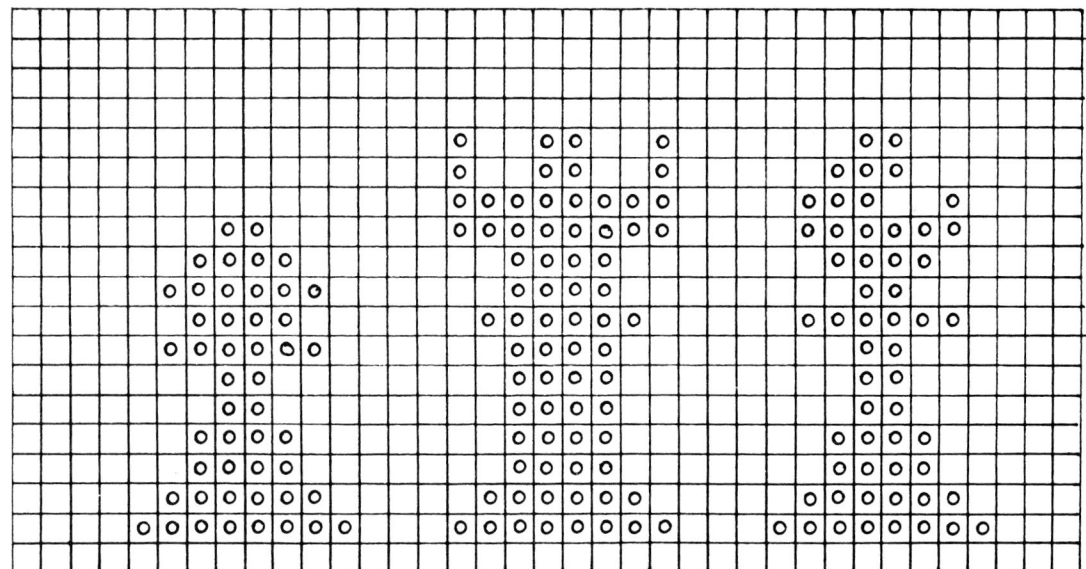

Next row: cast off 6(12) sts in self colour, work in correct colours to last 6(12) sts, place the 48 sts just worked on a holder, cast off rem. 6(12) sts.

Front
Work as for back as far as **.
Work 1(2) lines of complete squares on rem. 60(72) sts, but end with 15th row of check the last time.
Next row: ‡keeping pattern of checks correct, work 6(12) sts, turn and work on these sts only until front matches back to casting off. Cast off‡.

Rejoin yarn to rem. sts.
Work 48 sts, place these sts on a holder, work to end.
Still keeping check pattern correct, work as for other side from‡ to‡.

Sleeves
Make 2, in white.
Using smaller needles, cast on 43(45) sts.
Work 2in (5cm) in K1P1 rib as given for back.

Change to larger needles and st.st.
Inc. 1 st. each end of 7th and every foll. 5th(3rd) row until there are 71(95) sts.
Work straight to a total length of 13½(16)in, 34(41)cm.

Mark this point.
Work 2in (5cm) straight.
Cast off loosely.

Neckband
Join right shoulder seam.
Using smaller needles and white yarn, and with right side facing, pick up and K 23 sts down the left neck side; 48 sts from the front neck holder, working 2tog. in the centre; 23 sts up the right neck side, 48 sts from the back neck holder, working 2tog. in the centre (140 sts).
Next row: K1,(K1,P1) 33 times, K2tog., P2tog, (mark this st.), K2tog., P1,(K1,P1) 20 times, K2tog.,P2tog., (mark this st.), K2tog., (P1,K1) to last st., K1.
1st row: K1, (rib to 2 sts before marked st., P2tog., K1,P2tog.) twice, rib to last st., K1.
2nd row: K1, (rib to 2 sts before marked st., K2tog., P1,K2tog.) twice, rib to last st., K1.
Repeat these 2 rows of rib until 10 rows of rib have been worked in all.
Cast off in rib, dec. as before on this row also.

Making up
Join rem. shoulder and side seams matching squares and pattern. Seam sleeves as far as marked point, then insert sleeves so that rem. 2in (5cm) of sleeve fills the armhole shaping.

SLIPOVER

Back and front
Work as given for jumper, but work welts in black yarn; work neckband also as given for jumper, but in black yarn.

Making up and armbands
Join shoulder seam.

To make armbands:
Make 2, both alike.
Using smaller needles and black yarn, and with right side facing, pick up and K12 sts across the bottom of one armhole side; 36(48) sts up the armhole side; 36(48) sts down the other armhole side; 12 sts across the bottom of the other armhole side: 96(120) sts.
Next row: K1,(K1,P1) 4 times, K2tog., P2tog., (mark this st.) K2tog., P1,(K1,P1) to last 15 sts, working 2tog. in the middle of these sts at the shoulder seam, and therefore ending P1,K2tog., P2tog., (mark this st.), K2tog., (P1,K1) 4 times, K1.

Work 1st row and 2nd row of rib as given for jumper neckband until 8 rows of rib have been worked in all, casting off in rib on the last row, and dec. on the casting off row as before.
Make up rem. seams matching all colours.
Using the charts embroider in Swiss darning the chessmen in any positions you choose, using darker grey yarn on white squares and paler grey yarn on black squares.

PIECES OF EIGHT

The navy blue fisherman's jumper has been a favourite since Long John Silver knitted one, whether you call it a Gansey, a Guernsey or any of its other many names. This pattern has three extras: a simple Fair Isle yoke; an alternative dress version; and an optional detachable parrot! The dropped sleeves, moss stitch trim and side slits are all part of the tradition too, and, although the garments feel right in navy, pure wool, there is no reason why they shouldn't be in any other colour or yarn you like. (Picture p. 34)

Sizes
To fit chest 24(26 28 30)in, 61(66 71 76)cm.

Materials
For the jumper, in Patons Clansman double knitting: 6(7 7 8) × 50gm balls of navy yarn; 1(1 1 1) × 50gm ball of red, green and yellow yarns.
For the dress in Patons Clansman double knitting: 7(8 8 9) × 50gm balls of navy yarn; 1(1 1 1) × 50gm ball of red, green and yellow yarns. For the parrot: 1 Velcro spot fastener. Small quantity of washable stuffing.

Tension
24 sts and 32 rows = 4in (10cm) on size 8 (4mm) needles in st.st. over Fair Isle pattern.

JUMPER

Back
Using needles chosen for main tension, e.g. size 8 (4mm), and navy yarn, cast on 78(84 90 96) sts.
* Work 4 rows in K.
Next row: K.
Next row: K3,P to last 3,K3.
Repeat these 2 rows 3 times *.

Work in plain st.st., beg. K to a total measurement of 10½(10½ 12 12½)in, 27(27 30 32)cm, or desired length to armhole, ending with a P row.

To make yoke:
Work 6(8 10 12) rows in moss st.
Work 32 rows in st.st.
Work 6(8 10 12) rows in moss st.
Next row: Cast off 22(25 27 29) sts, work to last 22(25 27 29) sts, and place centre 34(34 36 38) sts just worked on to a holder, cast off rem. sts.

Front
As given for back as far as yoke.

To make yoke:
Work 6(8 10 12) rows in moss st.
Work 2 rows in st.st.
Work 29 rows from chart (opposite) in Fair Isle pattern.
Work 1 row in st.st.
Work 0(2 4 6) rows in moss st.

To shape neck:
Next row: Work in moss st. for 26(29 31 33) sts, work 2tog., turn, and complete this side first.
Keeping moss st. correct, work 2tog. on inside (neck edge) of next 5 rows.
Cast off.
Place centre 22(22 24 26) sts on a holder.

Rejoin yarn to neck edge of rem. sts, K2tog., work in moss st. to end.
Keeping moss st. correct, work 2tog. on inside (neck edge) of next 5 rows.
Cast off.

Sleeves
Both alike.

Using smaller needles, e.g. size 10 (3¼mm) and navy yarn, cast on 43(43 45 45) sts.
1st row: (K1,P1) rep. to last st., K1.
2nd row: K1,(K1,P1) rep. to last 2 sts, K2.
Rep. these 2 rows of rib until 2in (5cm) have been worked.
Change to larger needles.
Work 6(8 10 12) rows in moss st., at the same time, inc. 1 st. each end of every 6th(5th 5th 5th) row.
Change to st.st. and cont. to inc. 1 st. each end of every 6th(5th 5th 5th) row until there are 67(73 79 85) sts.
Work straight to a total length of

CHART FOR YOKE PATTERN

X yellow yarn
— red yarn
o navy yarn
/ green yarn

Rep. these 6 sts. throughout

11¾(12½ 13¾ 15)in, 30(32 35 38)cm, or ¾(1 1¼ 1½)in, 2(2½ 3 4)cm short of required length to underarm.
Work 6(8 10 12) rows in moss st.
Cast off loosely.

Neckband
Using back stitch, join left shoulder seam.
Using smaller needles and navy yarn, with right side facing, pick up and K34(34 36 38) sts from back neck; 6 sts down left front neck slope; 22(22 24 26) sts from front neck; 7 sts up right front neck slope: 69(69 73 77) sts.
Work 6 rows in K1,P1 rib.
Cast off loosely.

Making up
Press according to ball band instructions. Make up all rem. seams in back stitch matching bottom of moss st. band at back and front to the underarm, and leaving knitted border at bottom of side seams as an open slit in the traditional way.

DRESS

Back
Using larger needles, cast on 156(162 168 174) sts.
Work as given for jumper back from * to *.
Change to plain st.st.
Work 6(6 6 8) rows, beg. with a K row.
Next row: [K2togtbl, K48(50 52 54), K2tog.] 3 times.
Work 7(7 7 9) rows in st.st.
Next row: [K2togtbl, K46(48 50 52), K2tog.] 3 times.
Cont. in this way, dec. 6 sts on every 8th(8th 8th 10th) row, and working 2 less sts between decreasings each time, so working the decreasings above one another, until there are 78(84 90 96) sts.
Work straight to a total length of 16(18 19 20)in, 41(46 48 51)cm, or desired length to armholes, ending with a P row.

To make yoke:
As given for jumper back yoke.

Front
As given for dress back as far as armholes.

33

To make yoke:
As given for jumper front yoke.

Sleeves
As given for jumper.

Neckband
As given for jumper.

Making up
As given for jumper.

PARROT
Use needles chosen for main tension, e.g. size 8 (4mm), and st.st. throughout.

Body
Make 1.
In navy yarn, cast on 7 sts.
1st row: P.
2nd row: K, inc. 1 st. in every st.
Rep. 1st and 2nd rows once (28 sts).
Work 1 row.

Change to red yarn.
Work 2½in (6cm) straight.

Change to green yarn.
Work ½in (1½cm) straight.

Change to yellow yarn.
Work 1in (2½cm) straight, ending with P row.

Change to red yarn.
Next row: K3tog., K9, K2togtbl, K2tog, K9, sl.1, K2tog., psso.
1st row: P.
2nd row: K.
3rd row: P.
4th row: (K2tog., K7, K2togtbl) twice.
5th row: P.
6th row: K.
7th row: P.
8th row: (K2tog., K5, K2togtbl) twice.
Cont. working 1st to 8th rows, K2 less sts between decreasings on every 4th row, so losing 4 sts on every 4th row, until 10 sts rem.
Work ½in (1½cm) straight.

Change to navy yarn and work 1in (2½cm) straight.
Cast off.

Wings
Make one pair in yellow yarn, and one pair in navy yarn. In each pair, one is shaped the reverse of the other.
Cast on 3 sts.
Inc. 1 st. each end of every row to 11 sts.
Work straight to a total of 2in (5cm).
Keeping one edge straight, dec. 1 st. at other edge on every alt. row to 7 sts.
Dec. 1 st. each end of every alt. row to 3 sts.
Work 1 row.
Work 3tog., fasten off.

Wing patches
Make 2 in green yarn, 1 the reverse of the other.
Cast on 3 sts.
Keeping one edge straight, inc. 1 st. at other edge on every row to 7 sts.
Work straight to a total of 2in (5cm).
Dec. 1 st. each end of every other row to 3 sts.
Work 3tog., fasten off.

Beak
Make 1 in yellow yarn.
Cast on 13 sts.
Next row: K.
Next row: P.
Next row: (K1, K2tog., K1, K2togtbl) twice, K1.
Next row: P.
Next row: K2tog., K2togtbl, K1, K2tog., K2togtbl.
Next row: P.
Cast off.

Making up
Seam main body pieces into a tube and stuff, seaming tail end closed across with main seam central underneath. Seam a yellow lining inside each navy wing, matching all shapings and stuffing lightly. Stitch the green wing patches, one on each wing, matching the top shapings and padding slightly with stuffing. Attach wings. Seam the beak, stuff and attach open ended immediately below the navy stripe. Using black yarn, embroider feet on the yellow stripe. Using black yarn embroider nostrils, the beak line and eyes. Using white yarn, embroider a ring around the eye and a spot in the eye to give expression.

Use a silver or white sequin under a bead for the eye, and attach a velcro spot under the tummy.

35

PUPPY

It is always satisfying to carry a puppy in your jumper, after all the ancient Chinese carried Pekes up their sleeves! This seemed a little inconvenient, so this puppy is wrapped in his blanket, which happens to be the child's jumper. A blanket texture is suggested by the stitch and the edging is in traditional embroidered blanket stitch. The neck is fastened around Russian style at the side, with a neck tab at the shoulder. (Picture p. 39)

Sizes
To fit chest up to 26(up to 30)in, up to 66(up to 76)cm.

Materials
In Patons Beehive double knitting, 5(6) × 50gm balls of cream yarn. Scraps of maroon, black, white and small quantities of dark brown and pale brown yarns. 8 large press fastenings. Small quantity of washable stuffing. Length of ribbon.

Tension
24 sts and 32 rows = 4in (10cm) on size 8 (4mm) needles in st.st. On the same size needles the tension in pattern is 22 sts and 32 rows = 4in (10cm).

Stitch pattern
1st row: P1,K1,P1,*(K3,P1) twice, K1,P1, rep. from * to end.
2nd row: P1,K1,*P3,K1,P1,K1,P3,K1, rep from * to last st., P1.
3rd row: K4,*(P1,K1) twice, P1,K5, rep. from * to last 9 sts, (P1,K1) twice, P1,K4.
4th row: P3,*(K1,P1) 3 times, K1,P3, rep. from * to end.
5th row: as 3rd row.
6th row: as 2nd row.
7th row: as 1st row.

8th row: P1,K1,P1,*K1,P5,(K1,P1) twice, rep. from * to end.
9th row: (P1,K1) twice, *P1,K3,(P1,K1) 3 times, rep. from * to last 9 sts, P1,K3,(P1,K1) twice, P1.
10th row: as 8th row.
Rep. these 10 rows.

TO KNIT BASIC JUMPER

Back
Using needles 2 sizes smaller than those chosen for main tension e.g. size 10 (3¼mm), cast on 73(83) sts.

1st row: (K1,P1) rep. to last st., K1.
2nd row: K1,(K1,P1) rep. to last 2 sts, K2.
Rep. these 2 rows until 2in (5cm) of rib have been worked.

Change to needles chosen for main tension, e.g. size 8 (4mm) and stitch pattern.
Work straight to a total measurement of 17(19½)in, 43(50)cm, ending with a wrong side row.
Next row: cast off 26(29), K until 26(29) sts rem. Place the 21(25) sts just worked on to a holder, cast off to end.

Left front
Using smaller needles, cast on 53(53) sts work 2in (5cm) in K1P1 rib in the same way as given for back.

Change to larger needles and stitch pattern as given.
Work straight to a total measurement of 15(17)in, 38(43)cm, ending with a right side row*.

To shape neck:
Cont. to keep pattern correct.

36

Next row: ** pattern 13(11), turn and work on these sts only.
‡ Dec. 1 st. on inside (neck) edge on next 4(3) rows, then on each alt. row 3 times ‡: (6[5] sts rem.).
Work straight on these sts only until neck depth from the beg. of the neck shaping, measured straight, is 2(2½)in, 5(6)cm. (The total measurement of the work is now 17(19½)in, 43(50)cm.
Work a further 4 rows.
Cast off.

Rejoin yarn to inside edge of rem. sts, pattern 7(7) sts and place these sts on a holder, pattern to end.
Work as given for other side from ‡ to ‡: (26[29] sts rem.).
Work straight until this side of the neck matches the first side.
Cast off.

Right front
Work as given for left front as far as *.
Pattern 1 row, so ending at neck edge.

To shape neck:
Cont. to keep pattern correct, as for left front, from **, but cast off the 7(7) sts at the centre front neck, instead of placing these sts on a holder.

Sleeves
Both alike.
Using smaller needles, cast on 43(43) sts.
Work 2in (5cm) in K1P1 rib as given for back.

Change to larger needles and pattern.
Working all increases into the pattern, inc. 1 st. each end of every 5th(4th) row, until there are 71(83) sts.
Work straight to a total length of 12½(15)in, 32(38)cm, ending with a wrong side row.
Cast off.

Neckband
Carefully join shoulder seams in backstitch. Using smaller needles and with right side facing, pick up and K21(25) sts across back neck holder, 19(21) sts down the left side of the left front neck slope, 7(7) sts from the front neck holder, and 19(21) sts up the right side of the neck slope: (66[74] sts).
Cast on 7 sts at beg. of next row.
Work in K1P1 rib as given for back for 8(10) rows.
Cast off in rib.

Making up
Do not press. Make up side and sleeve seams in backstitch, and insert sleeves to give each a 7½in (19cm) deep armhole. In maroon double knitting yarn used double, work large [about ½in (1½cm) deep at ⅓in (1cm) spacings] blanket stitch down each front edge, excluding ribs and welts.
Fasten the 2 top neck strips, 1 inside, 1 outside, with the left front over, with large press fasteners. Invisibly sew 2 press fasteners to fasten the welt, then 1 at the opening edge 1½in (4cm) above the welt. Leave a 6in (15cm) gap. Then sew 1 more fastener. Space and sew 2 more between this and the top fastener. Finally put 1 on the collar.

PUPPY

Use needles as chosen for main tension and work in st.st. throughout.

Body
In dark brown yarn throughout, make 1.
Cast on 5 sts.
Next row: P.

1st row: (inc. 1 st. in every st.) to end, in K.
2nd row: P.
Rep. these 2 rows once.

Next row: (K1, inc. 1 st. in next st.) to end.
Next row: P.
Next row: (K1, inc. 1 st. in each of next 2 sts) to end: (50 sts).
Work 4in (10cm) straight, ending with a P row.

1st row: (K1,K2tog., K2tog.), rep. to end.
2nd row: P.
3rd row: (K1,K2tog.), rep. to end.
4th row: P.
5th row: (K2tog.), rep. to end.
6th row: P.

7th row: (K2tog.), rep. to end.
8th row: P.
Cast off.

Legs
Make 4, all alike.
In dark brown yarn cast on 12 sts.
Work 1in (2½cm) straight*.

Change to pale brown yarn.
Work ½in (1½cm) straight, ending with a P row.
Next row: (K2tog.), rep. to end.
Next row: (P2tog.), rep. to end.
Run a thread through rem. sts.

Ears
Make 2, both alike.
In dark brown yarn, cast on 10 sts.
Work 1in (2½cm) straight.

Change to pale brown yarn.
Work 2 rows straight.
Dec. 1 st. each end of every alt. row to 6 sts, then each end of every row to 2 sts.
Cast off.

Tail
Make 1.
Work as given for legs as far as*.
In pale brown yarn work 1in (2½cm) straight.
Dec. 1 st. each end of every other row to 6 sts, then every row to 2 sts.
Next row: work 2tog.
Cast off.

Head
In pale brown yarn*** cast on 5 sts.
Inc. 1 st. at right-hand edge of every row to 11 sts.
Work to a total length of 1½in (4cm), ending with a P row.
Leave these sts. on a holder***

Rep. from *** to ***, but make increases at left-hand edge instead.

With right sides facing, K across first piece, cast on 10 sts, K across second piece.
Work ½in (1½cm) straight on these 32 sts.

Change to dark brown yarn.
Work 1½in (4cm) more.
Cast off.

Making up
Seam the body into a sausage and stuff. Seam the legs into tubes and attach flat ended to underside. Fold the head in half and seam all pale brown and cast off dark brown edges. Stuff and attach open ended to top of body. Stitch on ears with a dart in the front brown part to give shape. Embroider features in black and white. Seam tail into a tube, stuff and attach flat ended in the obvious place! Stitch dark brown claws on paws and french knot the pad patterns. Stitch ribbon 'collar' around neck.
The puppy tucks in the 6in (15cm) gap in the front opening.

"THERE WAS AN OLD WOMAN..."

. . . who lived in a shoe . . . ' – in this case, on the front of a jumper! Finger puppets are easy to make, they are even easy enough for children themselves to learn to knit. The basic pattern here can be adapted for any characters you like, but these five finger puppets are all the children for the Old Woman, who is herself a glove puppet. They live in the shoe on this jumper, the pattern for which is useful for numerous double knitting jumpers and can be made in any colour that the prospective wearer prefers. (Picture pp. 42–3)

Sizes
To fit chest 24(26 28 30)in, 61(66 71 76)cm.

Materials
In Wendy Ascot double knitting, 5(5 6 6) × 50gm balls of grey yarn. Small quantities of brown, white, blue, green, red, yellow and pink yarns. 2 pieces of fine ribbon.

Tension
24 sts and 32 rows = 4in (10cm) on size 8 (4mm) needles in st.st.

TO KNIT BASIC JUMPER

Back
Using needles 2 sizes smaller than those chosen for main tension, e.g. size 10 (3¼mm), and grey yarn, cast on 79(83 89 95) sts.

1st row: (K1,P1) rep. to last st., K1.
2nd row: K1,(K1,P1) rep. to last 2 sts, K2.
Rep. these 2 rows until 18(20 20 20) rows have been worked.

Change to needles chosen for main tension, e.g. size 8 (4mm), and work in st.st., throughout. Work straight until work measures

10½(10½ 12 12½)in, 27(27 30 32)cm, or required length to underarm, ending with a P row.

To shape armholes:
Cast off 3 sts at beg. of next 2 rows.
Dec. 1 st. at each end of next 3(3 3 5) rows, then every alt. row until 61(65 69 71) sts rem. *
Work straight until armholes measure 5(6 6½ 7)in, 13(15 16 18)cm, ending with a P row.

To shape shoulders:
Cast off 6(7 7 7) sts at beg. of next 4 rows, then 7(6 7 7) sts at beg. of the foll. 2 rows.
Slip rem. 23(25 27 29) sts on to a holder.

Front
Work as given for back as far as *.
Then cont. straight until armholes measure 3½(4 4 4½)in, 9(10 10 11)cm.

To shape neck:
Work 24(25 26 26) sts, turn and complete this side first.
Dec. 1 st. at neck edge on next 3 rows, then every alt. row until 19(20 21 21) sts rem.
Work straight until armholes match those on the back, ending at outside armhole edge.

To shape shoulders:
Cast off 6(7 7 7) sts at beg. of next and every alt. row until 7(6 7 7) sts rem.
Work 1 row.
Cast off rem. sts.
Slip centre 13(15 17 19) sts on to a holder.
Work other side to match the first.

Sleeves
Both alike.
Using needles 2 sizes smaller than those chosen

for main tension and grey yarn, cast on 43(43 45 45) sts.
Work 18(20 20 20) rows in K1P1 rib, as given for back.

Change to larger needles and st.st.
Inc. 1 st. each end of 7th and every foll. 9th(7th 8th 8th) row until there are 59(63 65 69) sts.
Work straight until sleeve measures 12½(13½ 15 16½)in, 32(34 38 42)cm, or required length to underarm, ending with a P row.

To shape top:
Cast off 3 sts. at beg. of the next 2 rows.
Dec. 1 st. at each end of the next 5 rows, then every alt. row until 31(33 33 33) sts rem.
Dec. 1 st. at each end of the next 5 rows.
Cast off 5(6 6 6) sts at beg. of the foll. 2 rows.
Cast off rem. 11 sts.

Neckband
Join left shoulder seam. Using smaller needles and with right side facing, pick up and K the sts across the holder at back neck, working 2tog. at centre; 19(19 21 21) sts down left front slope; sts from front holder; and 19(19 21 21) sts up right front slope.
Work 2(2½ 2½ 2½)in, 5(6½ 6½ 6½)cm in K1P1 rib as given for the back welt.
Cast off very loosely in rib.

Making up
Join all rem. seams.
Turn the neckband on to the wrong side and loosely slip st. down.

SHOE

Make 1, in brown yarn, in moss st. throughout, using needles chosen for main tension.
Cast on 20 sts.
Next row: P.
Next row: inc. 1 st. in every st. (40 sts).
Cont. in moss st., inc. 1 st. each end of every row to 54 sts.
Work straight to a total length of 3in, (8cm).

Dec. 1 st. at right-hand edge of work 7 times.

Work one more row if necessary, to end at this right-hand edge.
Cast off 24 sts at beg. of next row, work to end.
Work 1 row.
Next row: work 6 sts, turn.
Work 2in (5cm) in moss st. on these 6 sts only.
Cast off.

Rejoin yarn to rem. 17 sts and work 2in (5cm) in moss st. on these sts.
Cast off.

OLD LADY

Main piece
Using larger needles and blue yarn, cast on 41 sts.
Work 4 rows in K1P1 rib, working 2tog. at the end of the 4th row.

Change to st.st. and work straight to a total measurement of 6in (15cm), ending with a P row.

Change to pink yarn.
Work 8 rows.

To shape head:
1st row: (K2tog., K16,K2togtbl) twice.
2nd row: P.
3rd row: (K2tog., K14,K2tog.) twice
4th row: P.
Cont. in this way, dec. by 4 sts on every alt. row until 20 sts rem.
Next row: (P2togtbl, P6,P2tog.) twice.
Cast off.

Arm
Using larger needles and blue yarn, cast on 3 sts.
Next row: P.
Cont. in st.st. inc. 1 st. each end of next and every alt. row to 17 sts.
Work straight to a total measurement of 3in (7cm), ending with a P row.

Change to pink yarn.
Work 2 rows.
Next row: K2tog., K4,K2togtbl, K1,K2tog., K4,K2togtbl.
Next row: P.

41

Next row: K2tog., K2,K2togtbl, K1,K2tog., K2,K2togtbl.
Next row: P.
Next row: cast off.

Apron

Cast on 30 sts in white yarn.
Work 4 rows in K.
Then work 2 rows st.st. starting K, 4 rows moss st., and 14 rows st.st. starting K.
Next row: (K2tog.) rep. to end.
Next row: cast on 50 sts at beg., work in moss st.
Rep. this last row once.
Work 2 rows in moss st.
Cast off.

Hat

Cast on 120 sts in white yarn.
Work 2 rows in st.st. starting K.
Work 4 rows in moss st.
Work 2 rows in st.st. starting K.
Next row: (K3tog.) rep. to end.
Next row: P.
Work 5 rows in moss st.

1st row: P.
2nd row: (K2tog.) rep. to end.
Rep. these 2 rows until 5 sts rem.
Run a thread through rem. sts.

CHILDREN

To make basic finger puppet:

Using needles chosen for main tension, cast on 12 sts.
Work 2 rows in K1P1 rib.
Work 18 rows in st.st.
Next row: (K2tog.) rep. to end.
Run a thread through rem. sts which can be used to seam up.

First boy

Work rib and first 6 rows of st.st. in brown yarn.
Then work 6 rows in white yarn.
Finish with 7 rows in pink yarn.

Second boy

Work rib in brown yarn.
In st.st. work 4 rows in pink yarn, 3 rows in green yarn, 5 rows in white yarn.
Finish with 7 rows in pink yarn.

First girl

Work rib and 4 rows in st.st. in pink yarn.
Work 9 rows in red yarn.
Finish with 6 rows in pink yarn.

To make skirt:

Cast on 24 sts in red yarn.
Work 2 rows in K.
Next row: P.
Next row: K.
Next row: P2tog. to end, casting off at the same time.

Second girl

Make as given for first girl, but substitute yellow for red yarn.

Baby

Cast on 10 sts in white yarn.
Work 14 rows in K1P1 rib.
In st.st. work 4 rows in pink yarn, starting K.
Next row: (work 2tog.) rep. to end.
Run a thread through these sts.

Making up

Fasten the shoe, centrally on the front, allowing the fullness to ease out (i.e. making a generous pocket). Attach by sides and bottom only. Then 'lace' the opening with ribbon (yellow) threaded through the edges of the shoe opening.
Embroider features and hair on finger puppets in any way you wish, stitching skirts on the girls. Embroider doors, flowers and windows on the shoe. Stitch seams to make up the Old Woman and seam and attach hat threaded with ribbon. Attach apron. Add grey hair and embroider features.
The toys can, of course, be stored in the shoe when not in use.

FLOWERS

This unashamedly feminine cardigan is made in luscious soft mohair colours and feels lovely. Do be careful that the all over Fair Isle pattern does not pull in the work and alter the tension. (Picture p. 46)

Sizes
To fit chest (24(26 28 30)in, 61(66 71 76)cm.

Materials
In Jaeger Mohair Focus: 4 × 25gm balls of pale green yarn; 1 × 25gm ball each of pink, lilac and pale pink yarns. Scraps of yellow double knitting yarn. 6 buttons of your choice.

Tension
15 sts and 20 rows = 4in (10cm) on size 5 (5½mm) needles in st.st. over Fair Isle pattern.

Back
Using needles 2 sizes smaller than those chosen for main tension, e.g. size 7 (4½mm), and pale green yarn, cast on 49(53 57 61) sts.
1st row: (K1,P1) rep. to last st., K1.
2nd row: K1,(K1,P1) rep. to last 2 sts, K2.
Rep. these 2 rows until 2in (5 cm) of rib have been worked.

Change to needles chosen for main tension, e.g. size 5 (5½mm).
Work 2 rows in st.st.
Work the 8 rows of the chart (see below) as given, with contrast as dark pink yarn.
Repeat the last 10 rows once.

From now on, work the colour sequence as follows and keep it correct throughout.
* Work 2 rows st.st. in green yarn.

CHART FOR FLOWERS

Back
1st row of chart: K.
Work 1(3 1 3) sts in pale green yarn, then rep. 8 st. rep. pattern until 0(2 0 2) sts rem., work 0(2 0 2) in pale green yarn.
Keep pattern correct throughout rem. rows.

Fronts
1st row of chart: K.
Work 4(1 2 3) sts in pale green yarn, then rep. 8 st. rep. pattern until 3(0 1 2) sts rem., work 3(0 1 2) sts in pale green yarn.
Keep pattern correct throughout rem. rows.

Sleeves
1st row of chart: K.
Work 2(2 3 3) sts in pale green yarn, then rep. 8 st. rep. pattern until 1(1 2 2) sts rem., work 1(1 2 2) sts in pale green yarn.
Keep pattern correct throughout rem. rows.

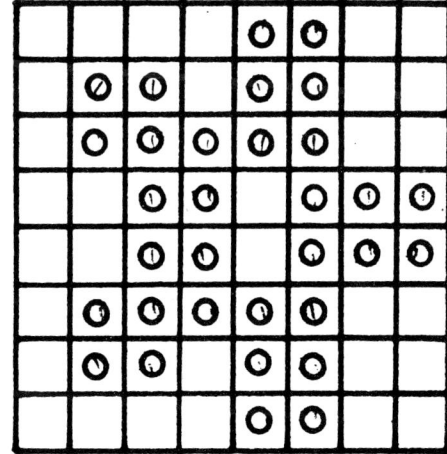

○ Contrast yarn
All rem. squares green yarn

Work the 8 rows of the chart with contrast as lilac yarn*.
Rep. from*to*once.
**Work 2 rows st.st. in green yarn.
Work the 8 rows of the chart with contrast as pale pink yarn**.
Rep. from**to**as necessary throughout the rem. of the piece of work. At the same time as the above colour sequence is worked, and keeping colours correct throughout all shapings, work straight until work measures 11(11 12½ 14)in, 28(28 32 35)cm, or required length to underarm, ending with a P row.

To shape armholes:
Cast off 2(2 3 3) sts at beg. of next 2 rows.
Dec. 1 st. at each end of next 3 rows.

For 2nd, 3rd and 4th sizes only:
Dec. 1 st. at each end of foll. 1(1 2) alt. rows.

For all sizes:
39(41 43 45) sts rem.
Work straight until armholes measure 5½(6 6½ 7)in, 14(15 16 17)cm, ending with a P row.

To shape shoulders:
Cast off 6(6 7 7) sts at beg. of next 2 rows, then 6(6 6 6) sts at beg. of foll. 2 rows.
Slip rem. 15(17 17 19) sts on to a holder.

Left front
Work throughout in colours to match the back.
Using smaller needles, cast on 29(31 33 35) sts.
Work 2in (5cm) in K1,P1 rib as given for back.
Next row: rib 6, slip these sts on to a holder, rib to end.

Change to larger needles and st.st.
Starting K, work straight in colour sequence until front measures same as back to armholes, ending with a P row.

To shape armhole:
Cast off 2(2 3 3) sts at beg. of next row.
Dec. 1 st. at armhole edge on next 3 rows, then on next 0(1 1 2) alt. rows: 18(19 20 21) sts.
Work straight until front is 9(11 11 11) rows shorter than back to start of shoulder shaping, so ending at front edge.

To shape neck:
Work 3(3 3 4) sts, slip these sts on to a holder, work to end.
Dec. 1 st. at neck edge on next 3(4 4 4) rows: 12(12 13 13) sts.
Work straight until armholes measure the same as on back, ending at armhole edge.

To shape shoulder:
Cast off 6(6 7 7) sts at beg. of next row.
Work 1 row.
Cast off rem. 6 sts.

Right front
Work throughout in colours to match back.
Using smaller needles, cast on 29(31 33 35) sts.
Work 4 rows in K1P1 rib as given for back.

To make buttonhole:
Next row: rib 3, yon, K2tog., rib to end.
Cont. in rib until 2in (5cm) of rib has been worked, ending at armhole edge.
Next row: rib to last 6, turn and place these rem. 6 sts on a holder.

Change to larger needles and st.st.
Starting K, complete as given for left front, but reverse all shapings, and end with a K row before armhole shaping.

Sleeves
Make 2 both alike.
Work throughout in the same colour sequence as back.
Using smaller needles, cast on 27(27 29 29) sts.
Work 2in (5cm) in K1P1 rib as given for back.

Change to larger needles.
Work 4 rows in st.st., starting K.
Inc. 1 st. at each end of next and every foll. 5th(5th 5th 5th) row until there are 37(39 41 43) sts.
Work straight until sleeve measures 13(13½ 14 15)in, 33(34 36 38)cm, or required underarm length, ending with a P row.

To shape top:
Cast off 2(2 3 3) sts at beg. of next 2 rows.
Dec. 1 st. at each end of next 3 rows.
Dec. 1 st. at each end on every alt. row until 21(21 21 19) sts. rem.

Dec. 1 st. at each end of next 3 rows:
15(15 15 13) sts.
Cast off 4(4 4 3) sts at beg. of following 2 rows.
Cast off rem. 7 sts.

Bands
To make button band:
Using smaller needles, cast on 1 st. and, with right side of left front facing, rib across sts on holder for front band (7 sts).
Cont. in rib until band, when slightly stretched, fits up front to start of neck shaping, ending with a wrong side row.
Break off yarn and slip sts on to a holder.
Sew band in place, stretching evenly and mark positions for 5 buttons, the first to match existing buttonhole in front welt and allowing for a 6th to be placed in 3rd row of neckband. Space the rem. evenly between.

Buttonhole band:
Work as given for button band, at the same time making buttonholes on right side rows to match markers as before.

To make neckband:
Slip sts from right front band and right front neck on to a smaller needle.
With right side of work facing, rejoin yarn and pick up and K11(13 13 13) sts up right front slope; K across sts on holder at back neck; pick up and K11(13 13 13) sts down left front slope; K across sts on holder at left front neck; rib across sts of left front band.
Work 4(5 5 5) rows in K1P1 rib as given for back, at the same time, making buttonhole as before on 2nd of these rows.
Cast off in rib.

Making up
Sew buttonhole band in place. Join side and sleeve seams. Insert sleeves. Sew on buttons. Embroider flower centres in yellow french knots.

DUFFLE COAT AND CAPE

Traditional duffles, in very small sizes, are rather stiff and unyielding, so here is a pattern for a duffle that is knitted in soft squashy yarn, but still has the traditional look, with toggles and a hood. The cape alternative is also made, in a broken rib stitch, which behaves well and does not curl up. (Picture pp. 50–1)

Sizes
To fit chest 20(22 24)in, 51(56 61)cm.

Materials
For the duffle coat in Patons Beehive Shetland Chunky, 6(7 7) × 50gm balls of red yarn. Small quantity of grey chunky yarn. 8 duffle toggles. For the cape in Patons Beehive Shetland Chunky, 5(5 6) × 50gm balls of red yarn. Small quantity of grey chunky yarn. 2 duffle toggles.

Tension
14 sts and 18 rows = 4in (10cm) on size 4 (6mm) needles in st.st.

Stitch pattern
*1st row: (K1,P1) rep. to end.
2nd row: (K1,P1) rep. to end.
3rd row: K.
4th row: K*.
Rep. from * to * throughout the work, as these 4 rows form the pattern.

DUFFLE COAT

Back
With needles chosen for main tension, e.g. size 4 (6mm), cast on 40(44 48) sts.
Work 2 rows in K.
Cont. straight in stitch pattern until work measures 11½(12 12½)in, 29(30 32)cm straight, ending with 2nd or 4th row of pattern.

To shape raglan:
Cast off 2 sts at beg. of next 2 rows.
Keeping pattern correct, dec. 1 st. at each end of every alt. row to 14(16 18) sts.
Work 1 row.
Cast off.

Left front
Using larger needles, cast on 28(30 32) sts.
Work 2 rows in K.
Change to stitch pattern and work straight until work matches back to beg. of raglan shaping, ending with a 2nd or 4th row**.
Keeping pattern correct, cast off 2 sts at beg. of next row.
Work 1 row.
***Dec. 1 st. at raglan armhole edge only of next and every alt. row to 19(20 21) sts, so ending at neck edge.

To shape neck:
Next row: cast off 8 sts, pattern to end.
Cont. to dec. at armhole edge on every alt. row as before, at the same time dec. 1 st. at neck edge on the next 5 rows.

For 1st size only:
Pattern 1 row.
Next row: K3tog, fasten off.

For 2nd size only:
‡Pattern 1 row.
Next row: K2tog., pattern 2.
Pattern 1 row.
Next row: K3tog., fasten off‡.

For 3rd size only:
Pattern 1 row.
Next row: K2tog., pattern 3.
Work as for 2nd size from ‡ to ‡.

49

Right front

Work as for left front as far as**.
Work 1 row.
Keeping pattern correct, cast off 2 sts. at beg. of next row.
Work as given for left front from***, so reversing all shapings.

Sleeves

Using larger needles, cast on 20(24 28) sts.
Work 2 rows in K.
Change to stitch pattern and inc. 1 st. each end of every 3rd(5th 7th) row, until there are 28(32 36) sts.
Work straight to a total length of 7½(9 10½)in, 19(23 27)cm.
Cast off 2 sts at beg. of the next 2 rows.
Dec. 1 st. each end of every alt. row until there are 4(4 6) sts.
Work 1 row.
Cast off.

Hood

Using larger needles, cast on 48(52 56) sts.
Work 2 rows in K.
Work in pattern for 7½(8 8½)in, 19(20 22)cm, ending with 2nd row of pattern.
Cast off.

Pockets (optional)

Using larger needles, cast on 16 sts and work in stitch pattern until work measures 4in (10cm), ending with a 2nd row of pattern.
Cast off.

Making up

Do not press. Join side seams, insert sleeves and attach hood after doubling and seaming the hood so that the cast on edge frames the face. The hood seam then matches the centre back neck. Attach the pockets, if made. Make toggle cords in grey (with twisted cords or plaits), attach, then sew on toggles to match.

CAPE

Back

Using larger needles, cast on 50(54 58) sts.
Work 2 rows in K.

Work in stitch pattern, working all shapings into the pattern.
Dec. 1 st. each end of every 10th row to 40(44 48) sts.
Work straight to a total measurement of 13(13½ 14)in, 33(34 36)cm**.
Dec. 1 st. each end of every alt. row to 30(32 34) sts.
Cast off 4 sts at the beg. of every row until there are 14(16 18) sts.
Work 1 row.
Cast off.

Left front

Using larger needles, cast on 33(35 37) sts.
Work 2 rows in K.
Work in stitch pattern, working all shapings into the pattern.
Dec. 1 st. at right hand (armhole edge) of every 10th row 5 times, at the same time, when the work measures 4in (10cm), ending with a wrong side row, work the foll. row to make the arm slit.

To make arm slit:

‡Pattern 12(13 14) sts, turn and work 4in (10cm) on these sts only, still shaping edge as before.
Leave these sts on a holder, pick up rem. sts.
Work straight until the second side matches the first side.
Work across all sts as before, dec. at outside edge only as before, until there are 28(30 32) sts.
Work straight until front matches cape back as far as*, ending at outside edge.
Dec. 1 st. at outside edge only on every alt. row 5 times.
Cast off 4 sts at outside edge of next 2 alt. rows, at the same time, when the front is 7(9 11) rows shorter than the back, cast off 8 sts at the neck edge, and dec. 1 st. at this edge on the next 5 rows, then work this edge straight until outside edge shaping is completed (2 4 6 sts rem.).
Work 1 row.
Cast off.

Right front

Work as given for left front, but reverse all

shapings, i.e. outside (dec.) edge is the left-hand edge, and work the arm slit row at ‡ as follows.
Next row: pattern 20(21 22) sts, turn.
Complete as for left front.

Hood
As given for coat.

Arm slit bands
Using needles 1 size smaller than those chosen for main tension, e.g. size 5 (5½mm), and with right side facing, pick up and K evenly 17 sts up the front edge side of the armslit.
1st row: (K1,P1) rep. to last st., K1.
2nd row: K1,(K1,P1) rep. to last 2 sts., K2.
Rep. these 2 rows twice.
Cast off in rib.

Making up
Do not press. Join side seams, matching all shapings and attach hood in the same way as for coat. Make a grey toggle cord and attach toggles to match. Catch down ends of arm slit bands.

KITTEN

This charming jumper will please any feminine feline fanatic and is made in brushed double knitting, which feels like a cat anyway. The jumper can be worked in all sorts of colours, and it would be fun, too, to make the cat a portrait of your own particular Felix. Striped and splodgy pompoms in the appropriate colours would transform this white Persian kitten into the ginger tom next door. (Picture opposite)

Sizes
To fit chest 24(26 28 30)in, 61(66 71 76)cm.

Materials
In Patons Promise brushed double knitting: 4(5 5 5) × 40gm balls of lilac yarn; 1(1 1 1) × 40gm ball of white yarn. Contrast chunky yarn with matching double knitting yarn for embroidery. Scrap of ribbon.

Tension
24 sts and 32 rows = 4in (10cm) on size 8 (4mm) needles in st.st.

Back
Using needles 2 sizes smaller than those chosen for main tension, e.g. size 10 (3¼mm), and lilac yarn, cast on 79(83 89 95) sts.
1st row: (K1,P1) rep. to last st., K1.
2nd row: K1,(K1,P1) rep. to last 2 sts, K2.
Rep. these 2 rows of rib until 18(20 20 20) rows have been worked.

Change to needles chosen for main tension, e.g. size 8 (4mm).
Work straight until work measures 10½(10½ 12 12½)in, 27(27 30 32)cm, or required length to underarm, ending with a P row.

To shape armholes:
Cast off 3 sts at beg. of next 2 rows.
Dec. 1 st. at each end of next 3(3 3 5) rows, then every alt. row until 61(65 69 71) sts rem. *
Work straight until armholes measure 5(6 6½ 7)in, 13(15 16 18)cm, ending with a P row.

To shape shoulders:
Cast off 6(7 7 7) sts at beg. of next 4 rows, then 7(6 7 7) sts at beg. of the foll. 2 rows.
Slip rem. 23(25 27 29) sts on to a holder.

Front
Work as given for back as far as *.
Cont. straight until armholes measure 3½(4 4 4½)in, 9(10 10 11)cm.

To shape neck:
Work 24(25 26 26) sts, turn and complete this side first.
Dec. 1 st. at neck edge on next 3 rows, then every alt. row until 19(20 21 21) sts rem.
Work straight until armholes match those on back, ending at outside armhole edge.

To shape shoulders:
Cast off 6(7 7 7) sts at beg. of next and every alt. row until 7(6 7 7) sts rem.
Work 1 row.
Cast off rem. sts.
Slip centre 13(15 17 19) sts on to a holder.
Work other side to match the first.

Sleeves
Both alike.
Using smaller needles and lilac yarn, cast on 43(43 45 45) sts.
Work 18(20 20 20) rows in K1,P1 rib, as given for back.

Change to larger needles and st.st.
Inc. 1 st. each end of 7th and every foll.
9th(7th 8th 8th) row until there are
59(63 65 69) sts.
Work straight until sleeve measures
12½(13½ 15 16½)in, 32(34 38 42)cm, or
required length to underarm, ending with a P
row.

To shape top:
Cast off 3 sts at beg. of the next 2 rows.
Dec. 1 st. at each end of the next 5 rows, then
every alt. row until 31(33 33 33) sts rem.
Dec. 1 st. at each end of the next 5 rows.
Cast off 5(6 6 6) sts at beg. of the foll. 2 rows.
Cast off rem. 11 sts.

Neckband
Join left shoulder seam. Using smaller needles,
and with right side facing, pick up and K the sts
across the holder at back neck, working 2tog. at
centre; 19(19 21 21) sts down left front slope; sts
from front holder; 19(19 21 21) sts up right front
slope.
Work 4 rows in K1,P1 rib as given for back.
Next row: K1, (rib 2, yon, rib 2tog.) rep. to end.

Next row: K.
Next row: K, inc. 1st. in every st.
Work 4 more rows in K.

Change to larger needles.
Work 2 rows in K.
Cast off.

Tail
Using larger needles and white yarn, cast on
28 sts.
Work 8 rows in st.st.
Cast off loosely.

Making up
Join all rem. seams. Using white yarn, make a
soft 4in (10cm) pompom and a soft 3in (8cm)
pompom and attach. Embroider paws, whiskers
and ears in white yarn. Seam the tail into a tube,
rev. st.st. side out, brush and attach. Attach
ribbon bow at neck. Using fine contrast yarn,
couch contrast chunky yarn into a squiggle and
the shape of a ball. Make a cord in chunky yarn
to thread through eyelet holes at the neck and
tie in a bow. For safety, firmly stitch this cord
centrally at the back neck.

SOFT TOYS

BEARS

Knitting teddy bears is a picnic! and the toys are a pleasure to live with. For the child they are charming and squashy, loving and comfortable; for the parents they are safe and washable. For a small baby it would be wiser to use any smooth yarn that works to the same tension, and for everyone, of course, make sure that everything is safe and non toxic. (Colour picture p. 58)

Sizes
The small bear is about 6in (15cm) high, and the large bear is about 24in (61cm) high.
NB Throughout the pattern, figures for the small bear are given first; those for the larger bear are in brackets.

Materials
In Sirdar Gemini double knitting: 1 × 40gm ball of brown yarn for the small bear; 5 × 40gm balls of orange yarn for the large bear. Short length of ribbon. 100(600)gm washable stuffing. 1 pair ³⁄₈in, (10mm) toy safety eyes for the small bear and 1 pair ¹⁵⁄₁₆in, (24mm) toy safety eyes for the large bear. Safety toy noses or buttons. Black double knitting yarn for embroidery.

Tension
22 sts and 30 rows = 4in (10cm) on size 8 (4mm) needles in st.st.
All pieces are worked in st.st. throughout.

Body
Make 2, both alike.
Cast on 8(32) sts.
Inc. 1 st. each end of every row to 16(60) sts.
Work 2(9)in, 5(23)cm, straight.
Dec. 1 st. each end of every row to 8(32) sts.
Cast off.

Legs
Make 2, both alike.
Cast on 14(56) sts.
Work 2(8)in, 5(20)cm, ending with a P row.
*Next row: (K2tog.) to end.
Next row: P.

For smaller bear only:
Next row: (K2tog.) to last st., K1.
Next row: P.
Cast off.

For larger bear only:
Next row: (K2tog.) to end.
Next row: P.
Cast off.

Arms

Make 2, both alike.
Cast on 2(4) sts.
Inc. 1 st. each end of every row to 14(56) sts.
Work 1½(4)in, 4(10)cm, straight.
Work as given for legs from *.

Head

Cast on 22(88) sts.
Inc. 1 st. each end of every other row to 30(124) sts.
Work 2 rows straight.
Dec. 1 st. each end of every row to 12(48) sts, then every alt. row to 2 sts.
Work 2tog.
Cast off.

Ears

Make 2, both alike.
Cast on 2(8) sts.
*Inc. 1 st. each end of every row to 6(20) sts.
Work 2(4) rows straight.
Dec. 1 st. each end of every row to 2(8) sts*.
Work 1 row.
Rep. from * to *.
Cast off.

Making up

Seam body pieces together and stuff. To make the head piece, bring the 3 main points of the head piece together to form the nose, and join the resulting Y shaped seam. Insert safety eyes and nose into head before stuffing. Attach arms to shoulders and attach legs with their top seams closed, so that they will bend at the join. Stuff head and attach at neck firmly. Double ears and attach at corners of head. Embroider features. Attach the ribbon bow, stitching it on firmly for a small child.

TORTOISE

Tortoises have tremendous charm, but they are about as cuddly as a well-done meat pie! This one is not only cuddly, but can be played with all the year round, and doesn't disappear into his shell when spoken to. He is quickly made in thick yarn and makes a very satisfying cushion or toy.

Size

The tortoise measures 18in (46cm) long.

Materials

In Wendy Shetland Chunky: 6 × 50gm balls of green yarn; 2 × 50gm balls of grey yarn. Scraps of black yarn. Approx. 1.7lb (750gm) washable stuffing.

Tension

14 sts and 20 rows = 4in (10cm) on size 3 (6½mm) needles in st.st.

Base

In green yarn, make 1 in st.st.
Using needles chosen for main tension, cast on 33 sts.
Inc. 1 st. each end of every row to 63 sts.
Work 5in (13cm) straight.
Dec. 1 st. each end of every row to 33 sts.
Cast off.

Sides

In green yarn, make 2, both alike.
Cast on 84 sts.
Work 4 rows in K.

Change to st.st.
Work straight until work measures 3in (8cm), ending with a P row.

59

1st row: (K2tog., K24, K2togtbl) 3 times.
2nd row: P.
3rd row: K.
4th row: P.
5th row: (K2tog., K22, K2togtbl) 3 times.
6th row: P.
7th row: K.
8th row: P.
Cont. in this way, rep. these 8 rows, dec. by 6 sts on every 4th row, and so dec. the number of sts worked by 2 each time between 'K2tog.' and 'K2togtbl' until 30 sts rem.
Cast off.

Legs
In grey yarn. Make 4, all alike.
Cast on 14 sts.
Work 3in (8cm) straight in moss st.
Next row: (K2tog., P2tog.) to last 2 sts, K2tog.
Next row: K2tog., P2tog., K2tog., P1.
Run a thread through these 4 sts.

Head
In grey yarn, make 2, both alike.
Cast on 20 sts.
Work 3in (8cm) in moss st.

Change to st.st.
Work 10 rows.
Next row: (K2tog) to end.
Cast off.

Tail
In grey yarn. Make 1.
Cast on 14 sts.
Work 2in (5cm) in moss st.
Keeping moss st. correct, dec. 1 st. each end of every row to 4 sts.
Run a thread through these sts.

Making up
Seam the sides together across top and down both ends. Insert base evenly between them and stuff firmly. Double tail and feet and stuff. Attach by their cast on edges on the bottom side seam so that they stick out flat, the tail centred on the back seam, and the feet in matched pairs. Seam the two head pieces together, leaving the cast on edges open. Stuff and attach open ended to the front. Embroider eyes and smile in black yarn, and toenails in single chains. Embroider outline squares on shell in grey yarn chain stitch.

Knitted cushions are extremely comfortable, and this one has the added attraction of doing something – it tells the time. The mobile hands can be used for teaching games, fun, or just for decoration, or, if you prefer your clocks always to 'stand . . . at ten to three', then the hands can be permanently attached at your favourite time. (Colour picture p. 58)

Size
The clock is approx. 15in (38cm) across.

Materials
In Sirdar Wash n' Wear Crepe double knitting: 4 × 40gm balls of yellow yarn; 2 × 40gm balls of white yarn. Scraps of black double knitting yarn and scraps of red aran or thicker yarn. Approx. 1lb (500gm) washable stuffing.

Tension
24 sts and 32 rows = 4in (10cm) on size 9 (3¾mm) needles in st.st.
NB Worked in st.st. throughout.

Back
Make 1.
Using needles chosen for main tension, e.g. size

60

9 (3¾mm), and yellow yarn, cast on 30 sts.
Inc. 1 st. each end of every row to 60 sts, then inc. 1 st. each end of every alt. row to 90 sts. Work 30 rows straight.
Dec. 1 st. each end of every alt. row to 60 sts, then dec. 1 st. each end of every row to 30 sts. Cast off.

Front

Work as given for back, but, after the first 16 rows, begin the white clock face by, from now on, working 12 sts in yellow yarn at the beg. and end of every row and all rem. sts in white yarn. Cont. in this way until work is 16 rows shorter than the back.
Work the last 16 rows in yellow only.

Edging

Using main size needles and yellow yarn, cast on 26 sts.

Work straight until work measures the same as the distance all around the edge of one of the main pieces when slightly stretched (i.e. approx. 45in (114cm).
Cast off loosely.

Making up

Seam the edging into a circle, then seam this in evenly around the edges of the front and back to give the cylindrical shape. Stuff before closing the final seam. Using thick red yarn, embroider a circle in chain stitch at the division between the white and yellow. Make a 10in (25cm) plait and attach it centrally to give one 4in (10cm) and one 6in (15cm) 'hand'.
Using black double knitting yarn, embroider the numbers in the traditional clock way, evenly spaced around the face. Each number is about 1½in (4cm) high and ½in (1½cm) from the edge of the white 'face'.

61

DIPLODOCUS

In this jumper any child can recite 'Hocus Pocus, I'm a diplodocus', because the main jumper is in the shape of a stylized dinosaur, complete with scales and spines (although Diplodocus probably had neither, never mind!). The back and front are alike, the jumper being worked in these two main pieces, which are worked upside down (the jumper not you!), so that the scale pattern looks authentic. Spines and cuff welts are added later. You may prefer to work in both directions and on a circular needle until the sleeves are completed, in order to accommodate the large number of stitches. The feet are loose over the welt, attached only by their claws. (Pictures opposite and p. 64)

Sizes
To fit chest 24–26(28–30)in, 61–66(71–76)cm.

Materials
In Wendy Shetland double knitting:
4(4) × 50gm balls of dark green yarn;
4(4) × 50gm balls of light green yarn;
2(2) × 50gm balls of black yarn. Scraps of red and white yarns.

Tension
24 sts and 32 rows = 4in (10cm) on size 8 (4mm) needles in st.st. over pattern.

Special abbreviations
DG = dark green.
LG = light green.

Scale pattern
1st row: using DG, P.
2nd row: using DG, K.
3rd row: using DG, P.
4th row: using LG, K3, * insert right needle tip into 3rd st. below next st. on left needle, draw up a loop, K next st., and pass the loop over the knitted st. and off the needle, K3, rep. from * to end.
5th row: using LG, P.
6th row: using LG, K.
7th row: using LG, P.
8th row: using DG, K1, rep. from * at beg. of 4th row, ending last rep. K1 instead of K3.
Rep. 1st to 8th rows as required.

Main pieces
Make 2, both alike.
Using needles (or circular needle) chosen for main tension, e.g. size 8 (4mm), and dark green yarn, cast on 215(263) sts.
Work in scale pattern to a total of 3½(4)in, 9(10)cm.
(NB Carry yarns loosely but neatly up the edge rather than breaking off each colour every 4 rows.)

To shape sleeves:
Keeping pattern correct, cast off 6(8) sts at beg. of next 16 rows: 119(135) sts rem.
Cast off 18(20) sts at beg. of next 2 rows: 83(95) sts rem.
Work 5½(7)in, 14(18)cm straight in pattern on these 83(95) sts.

To shape feet:
Next row: Pattern 6 sts, place them on a holder, pattern 24 sts., turn and work on these sts.
* Work 3in (8cm) straight on these 24 sts in pattern, keeping pattern correct.
Dec. 1 st. each end of next, then next 2 alt. rows (18 sts).
Dec. 1 st. each end of next 2 rows.
Cast off rem. 14 sts *.

Rejoin yarn to rem. sts.

62

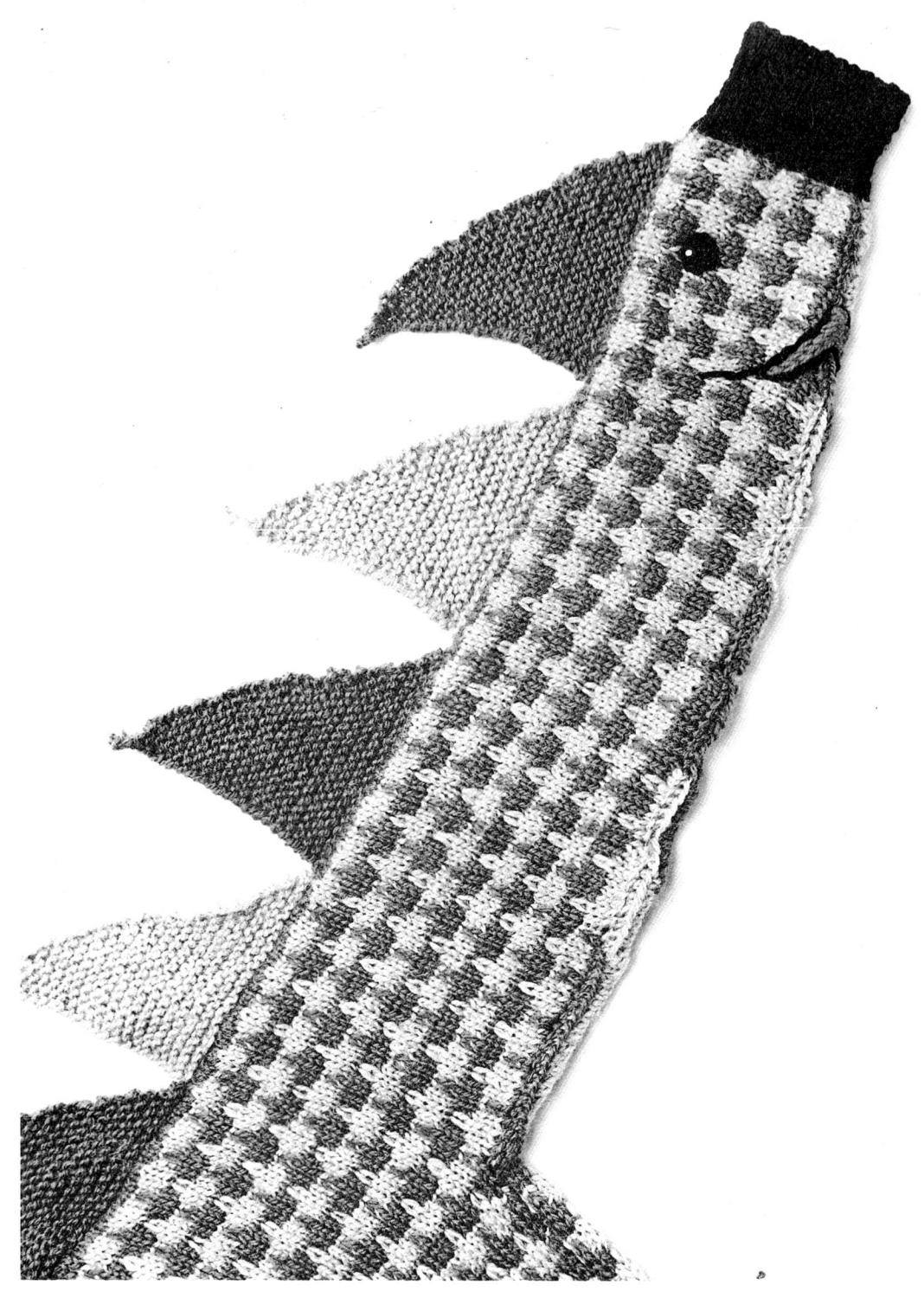

Pattern 23(35) sts, place them on a holder, pattern 24 sts, turn, placing rem. 6 sts on a holder.
Work on these 24 sts as for other foot from * to *.

Welt

Using needles 2 sizes smaller than those chosen for main tension, e.g. size 10 (3¼mm), and black yarn, with right side of work facing and with 'feet' at front of work, pick up and K6 sts from the holder at side of work, turn.
Cast on 24 sts, turn.
Pick up and K23(35) sts from the centre holder, turn.
Cast on 24 sts, turn.
Pick up and K6 sts from holder at other side: 83(95) sts.
1st row: (K1,P1) rep. to last st., K1.
2nd row: K1,(K1,P1) rep. to last 2 sts, K2.
Rep. these 2 rows in rib until 5in (13cm) have been worked.
Cast off loosely in rib.

Cuffs

Carefully join both shoulder seams, leaving, centrally, a 7½(8½)in 19(22)cm, neck opening.
Using smaller needles and black yarn, pick up and K, with right side facing, 43(49) sts, approx. 6 sts per 1in (2½cm).
Work 2in (5cm) in rib as given for welt.
Cast off loosely in rib.

Spines

Place the work flat and, except for the cuffs, divide the entire upper edge along the edge (i.e. the sleeve/shoulder seam and across the front neck) into 9(11) × 4in (10cm) sections.
A spine will be worked in each of these sections,

starting at the cuff with dark green yarn, then working alternately in light green and dark green yarns.

To make each spine:

Work throughout in K.
Across the marked 4in (10cm) section, using main needles and correct colour, pick up and K, as near to the shoulder seam as possible (or in one case at the neck edge, or in two cases both), 24 sts.
Keeping the left-hand edge of the spine straight (this edge to be the same for each spine), dec. 1 st. at the right-hand edge of every other row until 2 sts rem.
Next row: K2tog., fasten off.

To make spines for back neck:

Divide the rem. raw neck edge (i.e. the back neck) into 2 equal 3¾(4¼)in 10(11)cm, sections, and pick up 24 sts across each section, one in each colour.
Work spines as given above.

Neckband

Using a circular needle 2 sizes smaller than that chosen for main tension and dark green yarn, with right side facing, pick up and K46(50) sts across each of the front and back neck on the edge immediately inside the spines: 92(100) st.
Work 4 rounds in K1,P1 rib.
Cast off in rib.

Making up

Do not press. Join welts and cuffs in black yarn. Join underarm side seams carefully in backstitch in green yarn. Catch feet down by embroidering toe nails, embroider red smile and black eyes with a white dot in them.

HERE BE DRAGONS

Romantic doesn't really mean the sloppy bits in films, of course, it means adventure and mystery. So here is a romantic jumper with a fairy tale castle, a winding path and a cave, complete with a dragon (see chart opposite). The colours here are subtle and gentle but you could go for bright cartoon colours if you preferred. The dragon can be exotic or austere, funny or fierce, but, whatever he is, make sure, especially for a younger child, that all the decoration is safe, preferably embroidered, so that it can't be eaten. (Pictures pp. 66–7)

Sizes

To fit chest 24(26 28 30)in, 61(66 71 76)cm.

Materials

In Wendy Shetland double knitting: 3(4 4 4) × 50gm balls of turquoise yarn; 2(3 3 3) × 50gm balls of green yarn. Small quantities of grey, red, brown, heather and dark green double knitting. Scraps of white and yellow double knitting.

Tension

24 sts and 32 rows = 4in (10cm) using size 8 (4mm) needles in st.st.

TO KNIT BASIC JUMPER

Front

Using needles 2 sizes smaller than those chosen for main tension, e.g. size 10 (3¼mm), and green yarn, cast on 79(83 89 95) sts.

1st row: (K1,P1) rep. to last st., K1.
2nd row: K1, (K1,P1) rep. to last 2 sts, K2.
Rep. these 2 rows until 18(20 20 20) rows have been worked*.

Change to needles chosen for main tension, e.g. size 8 (4mm), and st.st.

For three larger sizes only:
1st row: K0(29 32 35) sts in green yarn, 20 sts in grey yarn, 0(34 37 40) in green yarn.
2nd row: P0(34 37 40) sts in green yarn, 20 sts in grey yarn, 0(29 32 35) in green yarn.

For two larger sizes only:
Rep. these 2 rows twice: (0[2 6 6] rows of st.st. in all).

For all sizes:
Beg. to work the chart with the first dark brown st. as the 25th(27th 30th 33rd) st. of this 1st(3rd 7th 7th) row and with the grey yarn 'path' matching previous rows on the 3 larger sizes.
Keeping the chart correct throughout all shapings, work straight to a total measurement of 12(12 12 12½)in, 30(30 30 32)cm, ending with a P row.
When the chart is completed, cont. in plain turquoise yarn.

To shape armholes:
** Cast off 3 sts at beg. of next 2 rows.
Dec. 1 st. each end of next 3(3 3 5) rows, then every alt. row until 61(65 69 71) sts rem. **
Work straight until armholes measure 3½(4 4 4½)in, 8(10 10 11)cm.

To shape neck:
Work 24(25 26 26) sts, turn and complete this side first.
Dec. 1 st. at neck edge on next 3 rows, then every alt. row until 19(20 21 21) sts, rem.
Work straight until the armhole measures 5½(6 6½ 7)in, 14(15 16½ 18)cm, ending at outside armhole edge.

To shape shoulders:
Cast off 6(7 7 7) sts at beg. of next and every alt. row until 7(6 7 7) sts rem.
Cast off rem. sts.

Slip centre 13(15 17 19) sts on to a holder and work other side to match the first.

Back

Work as given for front as far as *.
Change to larger needles and st.st.
Work straight until green yarn is the same length as the green on the front.

Change to turquoise yarn.
Work straight until back measures the same as front to armholes, ending with a P row.
Completing the back in plain turquoise, work as given for front from ** to **.
Work straight until armholes measure the same as those on the front to shoulder, ending with a P row.

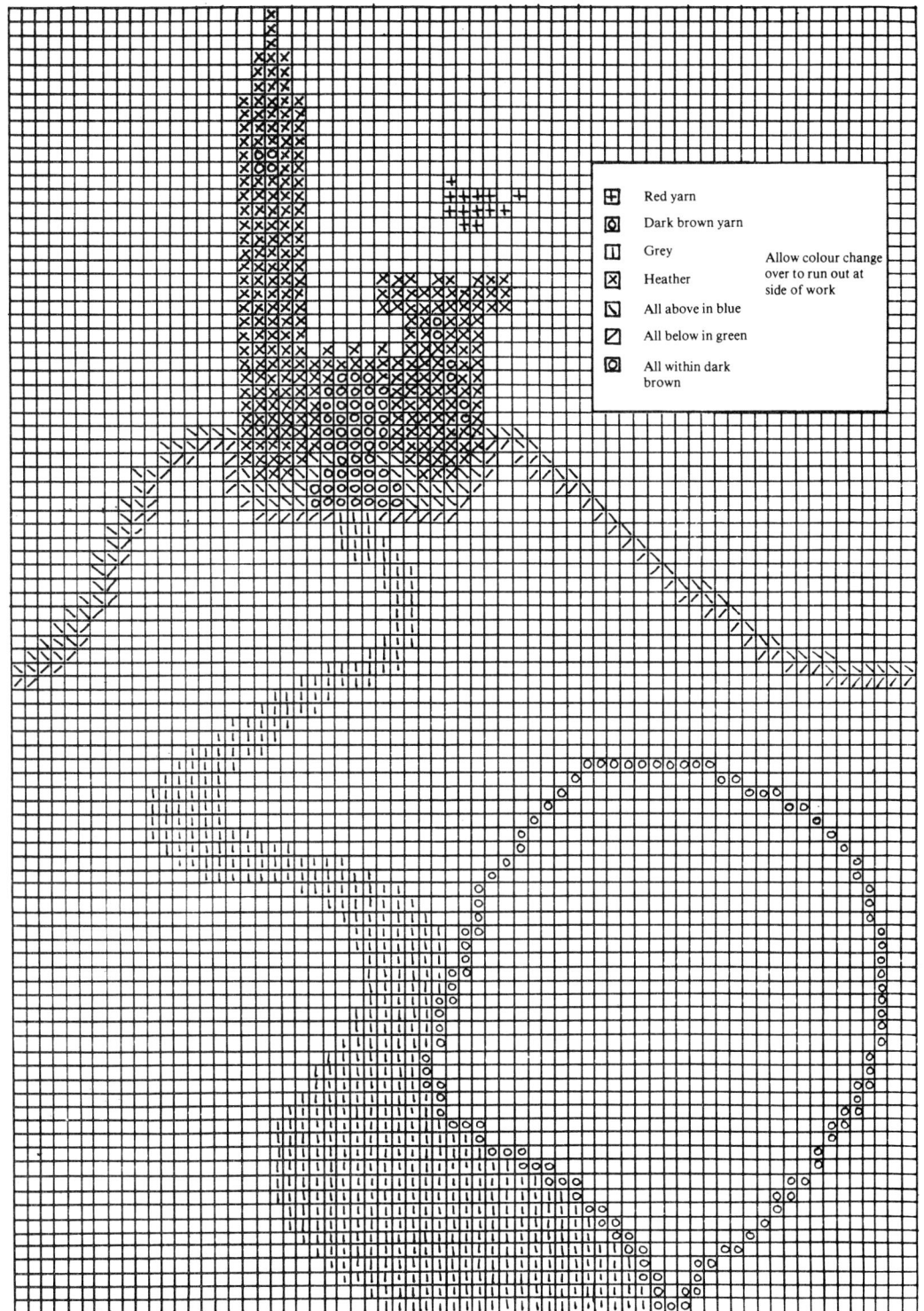

Red yarn

Dark brown yarn

Grey

Heather

All above in blue

All below in green

All within dark brown

Allow colour change over to run out at side of work

69

To shape shoulders:
Cast off 6(7 7 7) sts at beg. of next 4(4 4 4) rows, then 7(6 7 7) sts at beg. of the foll. 2 rows.
Slip rem. 23(25 27 29) sts on to a holder.

Sleeves
Both alike.
Using smaller needles and turquoise, cast on 43(43 45 45) sts.
Work 18(20 20 20) rows in K1,P1 rib as given for front.

Change to larger needles and st.st.
Inc. 1 st. each end of 7th and every foll. 9th(7th 8th 8th) row until there are 59(63 65 69) sts.
Work straight until sleeve measures 12½(13½ 15 16½)in, 32(34 38 42)cm, or required length to underarm, ending with a P row.

To shape top:
Cast off 3(3 3 3) sts at beg. of the next 2 rows.
Dec. 1 st. at each end of the next 5(5 5 5) rows, then every alt. row until 31(33 33 33) sts. rem.
Dec. 1 st. at each end of next 5 rows.
Cast off 5(6 6 6) sts at beg. of the foll. 2 rows.
Cast off rem. 11 sts.

Neckband
Press according to the ball band instructions. Join left shoulder seam. Using smaller needles and turquoise yarn, with right side of work facing, pick up and K sts across holder at back neck, working 2tog. at centre; 19(19 21 21) sts down left front slope; sts from front holder; and 19(19 21 21) sts up right front slope.
Work 2(2½ 2½ 2½)in, 5(6 6 6)cm in K1P1 rib as given for the front.
Cast off loosely in rib.

DRAGON

Main piece
Make 2.
Using larger needles and dark green yarn, cast on 22 sts.
Work 4 rows garter st.

Change to moss st.
Work to a total length of 7in (18cm).
Next row: K2tog., at each end of row.
Rep. this row until 4 sts rem.
Cast off.

Mouth
Make 2.
Cast on 22 sts in red yarn.
Work 6 rows in st.st.
Dec. 1 st. each end of every row until 4 sts rem.
Cast off.

CAVE POCKET

Make 1.
Using larger needles and green yarn, cast on 31 sts.
Work 32 rows in st.st.

Change to brown yarn.
Work 1 row.
Change to needles 2 sizes smaller.
Work 5 rows in K1,P1 rib.
Cast off in rib.

Making up
Make up rem. seams, matching colours. Attach pocket so that brown rib matches the cave 'mouth'. Seam the straight edges of the dragon, seam the mouth halves and insert, matching shapings. Embroider decoration on dragon and castle in any way you wish.

RAINBOW SETS

SHAWL

Size
The shawl is approx. 38in (97cm) square.

Materials
In Wendy Darling 4 ply: 3 × 20gm balls each of pink, apricot, yellow, pale green, pale blue, blue and lilac yarns.

Tension
28 sts and 36 rows = 4in (10cm) on size 10 (3¼mm) needles in st.st.

Lace pattern
1st row: K3, *yon, K2, K2togtbl, K2tog., K2,

yon, K1, *, rep. from * to * to last st., K1.
2nd row: P.
3rd row: K2, *yon, K2,K2togtbl, K2tog., K2, yon, K1, *, rep. from * to * to last 2 sts, K2.
4th row: P.
These 4 rows are repeated throughout the pattern as required, in the following colour sequence:
4 rows lilac
4 rows blue
4 rows pale blue
4 rows pale green
4 rows yellow
4 rows apricot
4 rows pink
These 28 rows are repeated throughout the pattern as required.

To make
Using needles chosen for main tension, e.g. size 10 (3¼mm), and lilac yarn cast on 256 sts. Work the lace pattern and the 4-row colour change sequence beg. lilac yarn and work straight until lace area is approx. square, ending with the 4th row of lace and after a lilac stripe.

* Change to garter st. (every row K.) and inc. 1 st. each end of every alt. row until there are 270 sts, at the same time changing colours every 2 rows in the foll. sequence: pink, apricot, yellow, pale green, pale blue, blue, lilac. Cast off loosely in lilac yarn *.
Along each of the rem. 3 edges, with right side facing, using needles chosen for main tension and pink yarn, pick up and K256 sts evenly (at the rate of approx. 7 sts per 1in (2½cm). Work as given from * to *, remembering that one row of pink yarn has already been worked.

Making up
Do not press. Join the mitred corners.

71

CHRISTENING GOWN

Sizes
Fits chest up to 19in (48cm); 28in (71cm) long.

Materials
In Wendy Darling 4 ply: 2 × 20gm balls each of pink, apricot, yellow, pale green, pale blue, blue and lilac yarns. 4 buttons of your choice.

Tension
28 sts and 36 rows = 4in (10cm) on size 10 (3¼mm) needles in st.st.

Back
Using needles chosen for main tension, e.g. size 10 (3¼mm), and lilac yarn, cast on 139 sts. Work the colour sequence as given for shawl (on p. 71), but work 2 rows per colour in K.

Change to lace pattern and 4-row colour sequence as given for shawl.
Work straight to a total measurement of approx. 24in (61cm), ending after a 4th row of pink yarn.

Keeping colour sequence in 4-row rep. correct throughout rem. of work and all shaping, change to st.st.

Next row: K1,(K2tog.) rep. to end: 70 sts.
Next row: P6,(P2tog., P5) rep. to last st., P1: 61 sts.
Work 6 rows straight.

To shape armholes:
Cast off 2 sts at beg. of next 2 rows.
Dec. 1 st. each end of next 3 rows: 51 sts*.
Next row: P.

To divide for back opening:
Next row: K28 sts, turn, K4, P to end.

To make buttonhole:
Next row: K to last 4, K2tog., yon, K2.
Work 17 rows more on these sts., keeping 4 sts in garter st. (all K) at inside edge, and making further buttonholes on 8th and 16th rows.

To shape shoulder:
Cast off 9 sts at beg. of next row and next alt. row, still keeping garter st. edge correct.
Work 1 row.
Leave these rem. 10 sts on a holder.

Rejoin yarn to inside of rem. sts, cast on 5 sts at beg. of next row.
Work to match first side, omitting buttonholes and reversing shapings.

Front
Work as given for back as far as*.
Work 19 rows straight.

To shape neck:
Next row: Work 18 sts, turn, and P back.
Cast off 9 sts at beg. of next row.
Work 1 row.
Cast off.
Slip centre 15 sts on to a holder.

Rejoin yarn to beg. of rem. sts.
Work 3 rows.
Cast off 9 sts at beg. of next row.
Work 1 row.
Cast off.

Sleeves

Make 2, both alike.
Keep colour sequence correct throughout.
Using main needles and lilac yarn, cast on 49 sts.
Work 3 rows in K.
Next row: P1,(P1, yon, P2tog.) rep. to end.
Cont. in st.st., starting K, for 14 rows.

To shape top:

Dec. 1 st. each end of every row to 29 sts.
Cast off.

Neckband

Carefully join shoulder seams in back st. Using needles one size smaller than those chosen for main tension e.g. size 11 (3mm), and lilac yarn, and with right side facing, pick up and K10 sts from holder at back left neck; 5 sts down left side of neck; 15 sts from holder at front neck; 5 sts up right side of neck; 10 sts from holder at back right neck: 45 sts.
Work 3 rows in K, making a buttonhole on the

second row in the same way as before.
Cast off loosely.

Making up

Do not press. Make up remaining seams. Stitch on buttons to match buttonholes.

LAYETTE

Sizes

Dress and jacket fit chest up to 18in (46cm).
Actual measurement 19in (48cm). Jacket, bonnet, mittens and bootees sizes as given.

Materials

In Wendy Darling 4 ply: 2 × 20gm balls each of pale blue, yellow, apricot, pale green, pink, lilac and blue yarns. 4 buttons for the dress; 1 for the jacket. 18in (46cm) of ribbon for the bonnet, 8in (20cm) each for bootees and mittens.

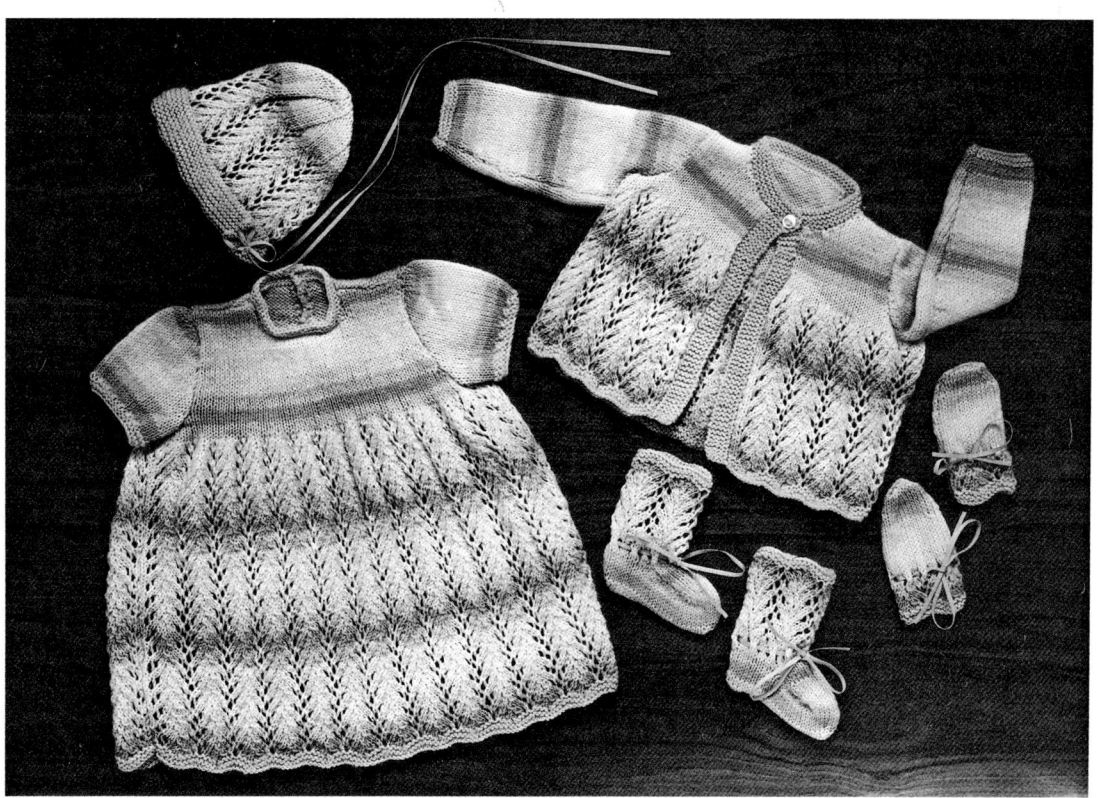

Tension

28 sts and 36 rows = 4in (10cm) on size
10 (3¼mm) needles in st.st.
NB Use the lace pattern and the colour
sequence as given for shawl on p. 71.

DRESS

Back

Using needles chosen for main tension, e.g. size
10 (3¼mm), and lilac yarn, cast on 121 sts.
Work 4 rows in K.

Change to lace pattern and colour sequence.
Cont. with blue, and working 4 rows per colour,
work straight to a total length of 10in (25cm),
ending with 4th row of lace pattern.

To shape top:

Keeping colour sequence (4 rows per colour)
correct, change to st.st.
Next row: K3,(K2tog) to last 2 sts, K2: 63 sts.
Next row: P*.

To shape armholes and divide for back opening:

Next row: Cast off 2 sts, K31, turn, K3,P to end.
Keeping 3 sts always in K at back neck opening,
dec. 1 st. at armhole edge on every row to 27 sts.
Work straight until back opening measures
1in (2½cm), ending at armhole edge.

To make buttonhole:

1st row: K to last 3 sts, yon, K2tog., K1.
2nd row: K3,P to end.
**Work 1in (2½cm) straight.
Make a second buttonhole by rep. 1st and 2nd
rows. **Rep. from **to **.
Work straight to a total measurement of
14in (36cm), ending with a P row.

To shape shoulder:

Cast off 8 sts at beg. of next and foll. alt. row.
Cast off rem. 11 sts.

Rejoin yarn to inside edge of rem. sts and cast
on 3 sts.
Keeping these 3 sts in K throughout, work to
match other side, matching colour sequence but
reversing shapings and omitting buttonholes.

Front

Work as given for back as far as *.

To shape armholes:

Keep colour sequence (4 rows each) correct.
Cast off 2 sts at beg. of next 2 rows.
Dec. 1 st. each end of every row until 51 sts rem.
Work straight until work measures 13in (33cm),
ending with a P row.

To shape neck:

Next row: K20, cast off 11 sts, K to end.
Working on this side only, dec. 1 st. at neck
edge on every row to 16 sts.
Work without shaping until armhole matches
that on the back, finishing at the armhole edge.
Cast off 8 sts at beg. of next row.
Work 1 row.
Cast off.

Rejoin yarn to rem. sts and work to match first
side, matching colour sequence but reversing all
shapings.

Sleeves

Make 2, both alike, ensuring both sleeves match
for colour.
Using larger needles and lilac yarn, cast on
37 sts.
Work 3 rows in K.
Next row: K6, (inc. 1 st. in next st., K1) to last
7 sts, K7.

Change to blue yarn (and so cont. colour
sequence at 4 rows each), and st.st.
Work 8 rows straight.
Keeping colour sequence correct, cast off 2 sts
at beg. of next 2 rows.
Dec. 1 st. at each end of next and every alt. row
to 23 sts.
Next row: work 1, (work 2tog.) to end.
Cast off.

Neckband

Join shoulder seams. Using needles 2 sizes
smaller than those chosen for main tension, e.g.
size 12 (2¾mm), and lilac yarn, and with right
side facing, pick up and K14 sts at left back
neck; 10 sts down left front neck slope; 11 sts at
neck front; 10 sts up right front slope; 14 sts at
right back neck: 59 sts.

Work 3 rows in K, making a buttonhole as before on the 2nd row.
Cast off.

Making up
Do not press. Join all rem. seams. Stitch on buttons to match buttonholes.

JACKET

Main piece
Back and fronts are worked in one piece.
Using needles chosen for main tension, e.g. size 10 (3¼mm), and lilac yarn, cast on 175 sts.
Work 4 rows in garter st.
Cont. in lace pattern, keeping colour sequence correct, until work measures 5in (13cm), ending with a 4th row of the pattern.
Next row: (right side facing) K1,K2tog., *K2tog., K2, rep. from* to end: 131 sts.
Next row: P.

To divide for back and fronts:
With right side facing and working in st.st., K28, cast off the next 6 sts, K63, including the st. on the needle from the casting off, cast off 6 sts, K to end.
Cont. on last set of 28 sts.

To shape left front:
Dec. 1 st. at armhole edge on next 4 rows, then on foll. alt. row once: 23 sts.
Work 12 rows in st.st., ending at front edge.

To shape neck:
Cast off 5 sts at beg. of next row.
Dec. 1 st. at neck edge on next 4 rows, then 1 st. on each alt. row twice: 12 sts.
Work 2 rows, ending at armhole edge.

To shape shoulder:
Cast off 6 sts at beg. of next row.
Work 1 row.
Cast off.

To shape back:
With wrong side of work facing, rejoin yarn to 63 sts.
Dec. 1 st. at each end of the next 4 rows, then on alt. rows once: 53 sts.
Work 23 rows in st.st., ending with a P row.

To shape shoulders:
Cast off 6 sts at beg. of next 2 rows, then 6 sts at the beg. of the foll. 2 rows.
Cast off rem. 29 sts.

To shape right front:
With wrong side of work facing, rejoin yarn to 28 sts.
Work to match the left front, reversing all shapings.

Sleeves
Make 2, both alike.
Match pattern and colour changes.
Using needles 2 sizes smaller than those chosen for main tension, e.g. size 12 (2¾mm), and lilac yarn, cast on 36 sts.
Work 4 rows in garter st. (all K).

Change to larger needles, and, keeping colour sequence correct throughout, inc. 1 st. at each end of next and every foll. 6th row until 48 sts.
Cont. in st.st. until work measures 6in (15cm), ending with a P row.

To shape top:
Cast off 4 sts at beg. of next 2 rows.
Dec. 1 st. at each end of every foll. alt. row until 34 sts rem.
Dec. 1 st. at each end of next 10 rows.
Cast off rem. 14 sts.

Front bands
Make 2.
Using smaller needles and lilac yarn, cast on 6 sts.
Work in garter st. until band reaches up front.
Leave these sts on a holder.

Neckband
Join shoulder seams. With right side of work facing, using smaller needles and lilac yarn, rejoin yarn to 6 sts of the right front band and K, then pick up and K60 sts evenly around neck edge, and K6 sts from left front band: 72 sts.
Next row: K.

To make buttonhole:
Next row: K2, yon, K2tog., K to end.

Work 3 rows in garter st.
Cast off loosely.

Making up
Make up rem. seams.

BOOTEES

Using larger needles and lilac yarn, cast on
40 sts.
Work 4 rows in garter st.
Then work in lace pattern and the colour
sequence as given until work measures approx.
2½in (6cm), ending with a 4th row of the
pattern.
Next row: K4,(K2tog., K4) to end: 34 sts.
Next row: P.

To make eyelet holes:
Next row: K1, * yon, K2tog., rep. from * to last
st., K1 ** .
Next row: P.

To shape foot:
Next row: K23, turn, P12, turn.
Working on these 12 sts only, work 16 rows in
st.st., starting with a K row.
Break off yarn.

With right side of work facing, rejoin yarn and
K 12 sts evenly along right side of instep, K12 sts
from instep, K12 sts evenly along left side of
instep, K11 sts: 58 sts.
Starting with a P row, work 7 rows in st.st.
Next row: K2tog., K25,(K2tog.) twice,
K25,K2tog.
Next row: P.
Next row: K2tog., K23,(K2tog.) twice,
K23,K2tog.
Next row: P.
Cast off.

MITTENS

Make 2, both alike.
Using larger needles and lilac yarn, cast on
31 sts.
Work 4 rows in K.
Cont. in colour sequence and work 8 rows of
lace pattern as given.

Change to st.st., keeping colour sequence
correct.
Next row: inc. 1 st. in first st., (yon, K2tog.) to
end: 32 sts.
Keeping colour sequence correct, work
2in (5cm) straight, ending with a P row.

To shape top:
Keep colour sequence correct.
Next row: (K1,K2togtbl, K10,K2tog., K1)
twice.
Next row: P.
Next row: (K1,K2togtbl, K8,K2tog., K1) twice.
Next row: P.
Next row: (K1,K2togtbl, K6,K2tog., K1) twice.
Next row: P.
Next row: (K1,K2togtbl, K4,K2tog., K1) twice.
Next row: P.
Cast off.

Making up
Make up all seams, matching pattern and
colours. Thread with ribbon. Sew button on the
jacket to match buttonhole.

BONNET

Using larger needles and lilac yarn, cast on
76 sts.
Work in garter st. for 16 rows.
Then work in lace pattern and colour sequence
as given until work measures 5in (12cm), ending
with a 4th row of the pattern, and dec. 1 st. at
end of last row: 77 sts.

To shape crown:
1st row: with right side facing, K8, * K2tog., K9,
rep. from * to last 3 sts, K2tog., K1.
2nd row: P.
Cont. to dec. in this way, working 1 st. less
between each dec. on next and every alt. row
until 14 sts rem.
Work 1 row.
Next row: K1, (K2tog.) 6 times, K1.
Break off yarn.
Thread through rem. sts, draw up and fasten
off.

Making up
Commencing at crown, sew up seam for
2in (5cm). Turn back the garter st. at beg. of
bonnet. Attach ribbon to the sides.

HOT DOG

This jumper has food all down the front, and no one minds! The chequered tablecloth is a very cunning piece of picture knitting, and you may prefer to leave it at that. Or, just for fun, add the simple hot dog, with mustard, lettuce or any other garnish you like – ketchup, perhaps, or onions. (Picture p. 82)

Sizes
To fit chest 24(26 28 30)in, 61(66 71 76)cm.

Materials
In Sirdar Wash 'n Wear double crepe:
2(3 3 3) × 40gm balls of red yarn;
4(5 5 5) × 40gm balls of white yarn. Small quantities of pale brown, dark brown, yellow, blue and green yarns. Small quantity of washable toy stuffing.

Tension
24 sts and 32 rows = 4in (10cm) on size 9 (3¾mm) needles in st.st.

TO KNIT BASIC JUMPER

Back
Using needles 2 sizes smaller than those chosen for main tension, e.g. size 11 (3mm), and red yarn, cast on 79(85 91 97) sts.
1st row: (K1,P1) rep. to last st., K1.
2nd row: K1,(K1,P1) rep. to last 2 sts, K2.
Rep. these 2 rows until 2in (5cm) have been worked.

Change to needles chosen for main tension, e.g. size 9 (3¾mm), and st.st.
Work from the chart opposite to the beg. of the raglan shaping, so ending with a P row.
Cont. to keep chart correct, cast off 3 sts at beg. of next 2 rows.

To shape raglan:
1st row: K2,K2togtbl, K to last 4 sts, K2tog., K2.
2nd row: K1,P to last st., K1*.
Rep. these 2 rows until 27(31 35 41) sts rem.

For 1st and 2nd sizes only:
Place these sts on a holder.

For 3rd and 4th sizes only:
Dec. as before, but on every 4th row until 33(35) sts rem.
Place these sts on a holder.

Front
Work as given for back as far as *.
Rep. 1st and 2nd raglan rows until 43(47 51 57) sts rem., ending with a P row.

To shape neck:
Next row: K2,K2togtbl, K11(12 13 16), turn, P2tog., P to last st., K1.
Work on these sts only.
**Cont. to dec. on raglan edge as before on next, then every alt. row 5 times; at the same time, dec. 1 st. at neck edge on next 1(2 3 6) rows, then on every alt. row twice, then work this edge straight until alt. raglan dec. is completed (4 sts. rem.), ending with a P row.
Next row: K2,K2togtbl.
Next row: P.
Next row: K1,K2togtbl.
Next row: P2tog., fasten off**.
Place centre 13(15 17 17) sts on a holder.

Rejoin yarn to rem. sts.
Next row: K to last 4, K2tog., K2.
Next row: K1,P to last 2 sts, P2tog.
Work as given for other side from ** to **.

Sleeves
Both alike, in white.

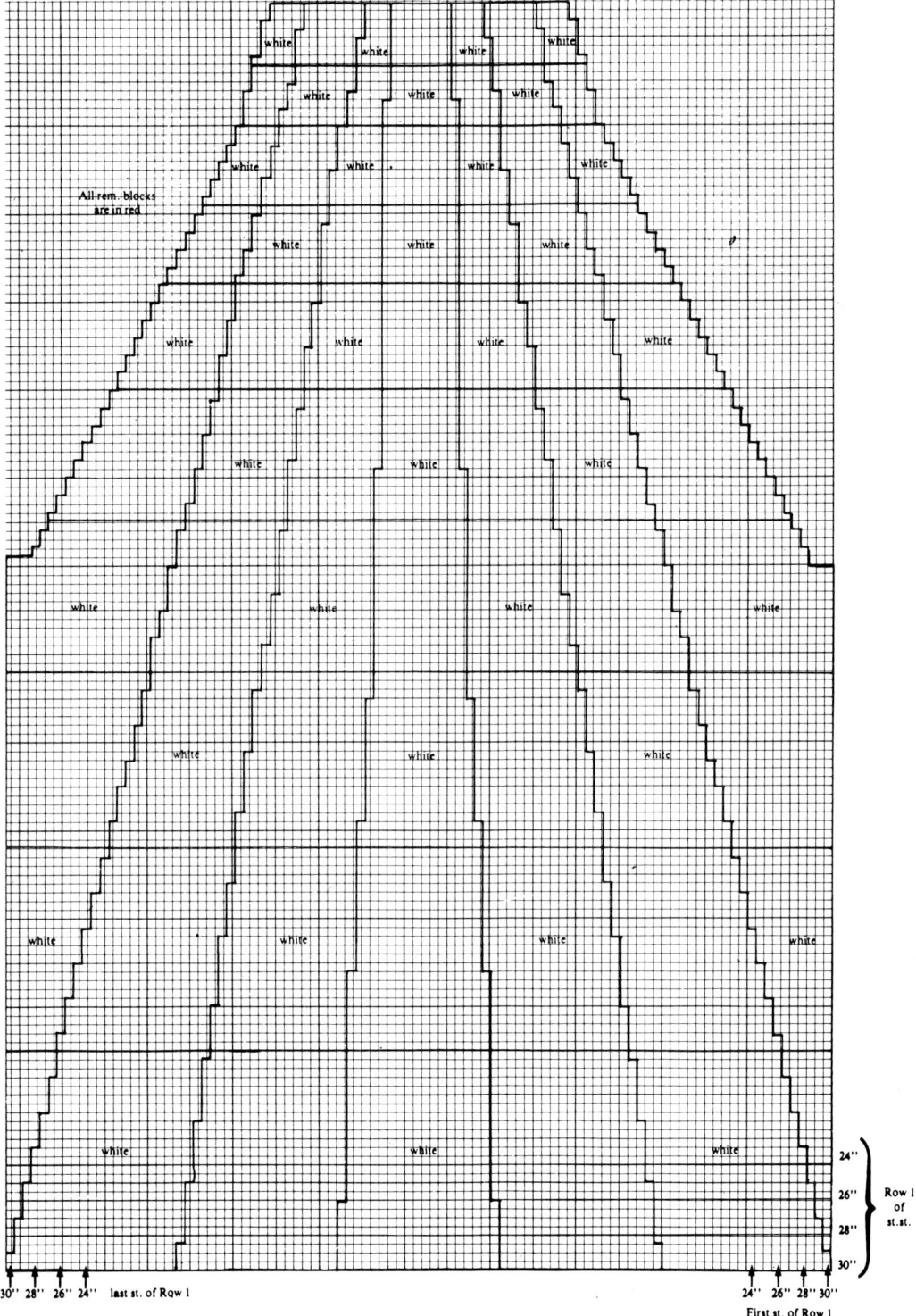

All rem. blocks
are in red

white white white white

white white white

white white white white

white white white

white white white white

white white white

white white white white

white white white

white white white white

white white white

white white white

24"

26"

28"

30"

} Row 1 of st.st.

30" 28" 26" 24" last st. of Row 1

24" 26" 28" 30"

First st. of Row 1

81

Using smaller needles, cast on 35(39 43 47) sts. Work 2in (5cm) in K1,P1 rib as given for back.

Change to larger needles and st.st.
Next row: K4(6 8 6) sts, (inc. 1 st. in next st., K9) 3 times, inc. 1 st. in next st., K to end: 39(43 47 51) sts.
Cont. in st.st. inc. 1 st. each end of every 6th row until there are 61(67 73 79) sts.
Work straight to a total measurement of 13(13 15 16)in, 33(33 38 41)cm, or required measurement to underarm, ending with a P row.
Cast off 3 sts at beg. of next 2 rows.
Dec. for raglan on every other row as given for back, until 11(11 11 13) sts rem.
Cont. to dec. but on every 4th row, until 9(9 9 9) sts rem.
Work 1 row.
Leave these sts on a holder.

Neckband

Do not press. Join both front and back left raglan seams in backstitch. Using red yarn and smaller needles, and with right side facing, pick up and K27(31 33 35) sts from the back neck holder, 9 sts from the left sleeve holder; 10(10 10 10) sts down the left front neck slope; 13(15 17 17) sts from the front neck holder; 10(10 10 10) sts up the right neck slope; 9 sts from the right sleeve holder: 78(84 88 90) sts.

Rep. the rib rows as given for back until a total of 2(2 2½ 2½)in, 5(5 6 6)cm of rib has been worked.
Cast off loosely in rib.

Making up

Do not press. Join all rem. seams carefully in backstitch, matching squares where possible. Turn neckband on to wrong side and loosely slip st. down.

PLATE

In white yarn, in st.st. throughout on larger needles.
Cast on 42 sts.
Next row: P.
Cont. in st.st. inc. 1 st. each end of every row 6 times: (54 sts); then every alt. row 3 times: (60 sts).
Work 16 rows straight.
Dec. 1 st. each end of next then every alt. row twice: (54 sts); then every row 6 times: (42 sts).
Work 1 row.
Cast off.

BREAD BUN

In pale brown yarn in st.st. throughout on larger needles.
Cast on 32 sts.
Next row: P.
Cont. in st.st. inc. 1 st. each end of every row 6 times: (44 sts); then every alt. row 3 times: (50 sts).
Work 16 rows straight.
Dec. 1 st. each end of next then every alt. row twice: (44 sts); then every row 6 times: (32 sts).
Work 1 row.
Cast off.

SAUSAGE

In dark brown yarn, in st.st. throughout on larger needles.
Cast on 55 sts.
Work 2in (5cm) straight.
Cast off loosely.

Making up the pieces of food

Attach plate centrally and embroider blue stripes. Seam and stuff sausage and attach over bread bun, then pad the bread bun and attach. Embroider seeds on bun top and mustard with chain stitch. Embroider cucumber.

HAT AND SCARF SETS

Hats, scarves and gloves are much less likely to be lost, and, if lost, much more likely to be found, if they are fun to wear, and do things. So here are spiders in webs and ghosts in haunted houses for little horrors to terrorize the district in, and, for the storyteller in the family, Punch and Judy belong in their booths and can tell the traditional story to brighten a cold day's walk. (Pictures pp. 86–7)

Materials
In Wendy Ascot double knitting, each set takes 4 × 50gm balls of main colour yarn, with scraps of the additional colours. Buttons and bells.

Tension
24 sts and 32 rows = 4in (10cm) on size 8 (4mm) needles in st.st.

BASIC PATTERNS FOR ALL SETS

Right mitten
Using needles 2 sizes smaller than those for main tension, e.g. size 10 (3¼mm), cast on 37 sts.
1st row: (K1,P1) rep. to last st., K1.
2nd row: K1,(K1,P1) rep. to last 2 sts, K2.
Rep. these 2 rows in rib until 2in (5cm) have been worked.

To make thumb:
Change to larger needles, e.g. size 8 (4mm) and st.st.
1st row: K19, inc. 1 st. in next st., K2, inc. 1 st. in next st., K to end.
2nd row: P.
3rd row: K.
4th row: P.
5th row: K19, inc. 1 st. in next st., K4, inc. 1 st. in next st., K to end.
6th row: P.
7th row: K.
8th row: P.

Cont. in this way, inc. by 2 sts, 1 each side of the thumb, on every 4th row, until there are 10 sts between the increases.
Work 1 row.

To divide for thumb:
Next row: K30, turn, P10, turn.
Next row: Cast on 2 sts at beg. of row.
Work 10 rows on these 12 sts, so ending with a P row.

To shape top:
Next row: (K2tog.) 6 times.
Next row: P.
Next row: (K2tog) 3 times, run a thread through rem. sts.

Rejoin yarn to edge of 2 cast on sts at base of thumb, pick up these 2 sts and K them, K to end (39 sts).
* Work 14 rows.

To shape top:
Next row: (K1,K2togtbl, K14,K2tog.) twice, K1.
Next row: P.
Next row: (K1,K2togtbl, K12,K2tog.) twice, K1.
Next row: P.
Next row: (K1,K2togtbl, K10,K2tog.) twice, K1.
Next row: P.
Cast off.

Left mitten
Using smaller needles, cast on 37 sts.
Work 2in (5cm) in K1P1 rib as given for right mitten.

To make thumb:
Change to larger needles and st.st.

84

1st row: K14, inc. 1 st. in next st., K2, inc. 1 st. in next st., K to end.
Cont. as given for right mitten, but using this foundation row to reverse all shaping and inc. on every 4th row in the same way until there are 10 sts between increasings.
Work 1 row.

To divide for thumb:
Next row: K25, cast on 2, turn, P12.
Cont. for thumb as given on right mitten.
Complete mitten as given for right mitten to match.

Scarf
Using needles chosen for main tension, cast on 53 sts.
Work in K1,P1 rib, as given for mittens, to a total of 40in (102cm).
Cast off in rib.

Hat
Using smaller needles cast on 121 sts.
Work 2in (5cm) in K1,P1 rib as given for mittens.

Change to larger needles and keep rib correct.
Work to a total length of 5½in (14cm), ending so that the next row should beg. K1,P1; but instead work as follows:
1st row: P2tog., rib 37, P3tog., rib 37, P3tog., rib 37, P2tog.
2nd row: rib.
3rd row: K2tog., rib 35, K3tog., rib 35, K3tog., rib 35, K2tog.
4th row: rib.
Cont. in this way, but dec. by 6 sts on every alt. row and keep rib correct to 43 sts.
Next row: rib.
Next row: K1,(K2tog.) to end.
Run a thread through rem. sts and use this thread to seam the hat together.

SPIDERS

Mittens
Make in white yarn throughout. Attach 3in (8cm) leg plaits and firm 1½in (4cm) black pompoms centrally to the back of each hand.

Scarf
Make in white yarn. Add 3in (8cm) pompoms to the gathered ends in black yarn and embroider a black spider's web.

Hat
Make in white yarn throughout. Then attach 4 × 4in (10cm) black plaits centrally to make 8 legs. Make a firm 3in (8cm) diameter pompom in black yarn and attach over the legs.

GHOSTS

Mittens
In white yarn throughout. Embroider black 'ghostly' faces.

Scarf
Make in maroon yarn. Fringe ends with pale green and black yarns alternately.

To make haunted house pockets:
Make 2, both alike, in st.st.
Using larger needles and pale green yarn, cast on 25 sts.
Work 6in (15cm) straight.

Change to black yarn.
Work 2 rows.

Change to pale green yarn.
Dec. 1 st. each end of every alt. row to 3 sts.
Work 1 row.
Next row: slip 1, K2tog., psso.
Fasten off.

To make haunted house door:
Make 2, both alike, in st.st.
Using larger needles and black yarn, cast on 15 sts.
Work 4½in (11cm) straight.
Dec. 1 st. each end of every row to 5 sts.
Cast off.
Attach doors to houses and attach houses as pockets to scarf ends, attaching roof by centre point only.

Hat
Work 2in (5cm) in pale green yarn. Complete in maroon yarn. Add a firm 3in (8cm) diameter pompom in black and white patches.

PUNCH AND JUDY

Mittens
Make 1 as Punch, 1 as Judy.

To make Punch:
Using larger needles and in red yarn, cast on 37 sts.
Work 4 rows in K.

Change to smaller needles, rib and dark green yarn.
Cont. working: all rib in green yarn; thumb and all shaping at base and first 10 rows of the st.st. at * in pink yarn; rem. 4 straight rows in red yarn; and all end shaping in green yarn.
Embroider features and stitch on buttons. Add a bell to the top of the hat.

To make Judy:
Cast on and K4 rows as given for Punch, but in white yarn.
Work the rib in blue yarn. Then work pink yarn as given for Punch and all rem. in white yarn.

To make a hat frill:
Using main size needles, cast on 78 sts.
Work 6 rows in K.
Next row: K2tog. to end.
Next row: K1, (yon, K2tog.) to end.
Next row: K.
Cast off.
After the mitten is made up stitch this frill around the line where the white top of the mitten begins. Embroider features. Add yellow plaits under the hat brims, thread a multi-coloured plait around the hat.

Scarf
Work in 8 row stripes of red and dark green yarns, beg. and ending the scarf with a red stripe. Fringe ends in red yarn.

To make tent pockets:
Make 2.
Using main size needles and white yarn, cast on 30 sts.
Work straight in st.st. to a total length of 5in (13cm), ending with a P row.
Next row: K5, turn.
Work 2in (5cm) on these 5 sts only, ending with a P row.

Rejoin yarn to rem. sts, cast off centre 20 sts.
Work 2in (5cm) on rem. 5 sts, ending with a P row.
Work across the first 5 sts, keeping st.st. correct cast on 20 sts. in the centre, and work across the other 5 sts.
Work ¾in (2cm) in st.st., ending with a P row.
Next row: K1 (yon, K2tog.) to last st. K1.
Next row: P.
Next row: K.
Next row: P.
Cast off.
Attach tent pockets to end of scarf, leaving the bottom edge only of the central hole open as the pocket top. Embroider a row of alternate red and green French knots along this edge.

Hat
Work the first 2in (5cm) in red yarn, and rem. in green yarn. Add a firm 3in (8cm) red pompom.

TRAIN-SPOTTING

This jumper, for a young steam fanatic, provides the owner with a personalised train-track layout, complete with train. The tracks (see chart below) go completely around the jumper and into the tunnel, and the simple toy train is made separately. The pocket is also useful for sweets, hankies and other essential train-spotting equipment. (Pictures p. 91 and p. 92)

Sizes
To fit chest 24(26 28 30)in, 61(66 71 76)cm.

Materials
In Sirdar Wash n' Wear Aran: 6(7 7 8) × 50gm balls of blue yarn; 2(2 2 3) × 50gm balls of green yarn; 1 × 50gm ball of grey yarn; 1 × 50gm ball of brown yarn; 1 × 50gm ball of red yarn. Scraps of black, yellow and white double knitting yarns. A small quantity of washable stuffing.

Tension
19 sts and 25 rows = 4in (10cm) on size 7 (4½mm) needles in st.st.

TO KNIT BASIC JUMPER

Back
Using needles 2 sizes smaller than those chosen for main tension, e.g. size 9 (3¾mm), and green yarn, cast on 61(67 71 77) sts.
1st row: (K1,P1) to last st., K1.
2nd row: K1,(K1,P1) to last 2 sts, K2.
Rep. these 2 rows of rib until 2in (5cm) have been worked.

Change to larger needles, e.g. size 7 (4½mm) and st.st.
Work 9 rows beginning K.
Change to grey yarn.
Next row: P.
Work the 'railway lines' from the chart below.
Then work 1 row in grey yarn.
Change to green yarn, work to a total length from the cast on edge of 7in (18cm).

Change to blue yarn.
Work straight to a total measurement of 10½(10½ 12 12½)in, 27(27 30 32)cm, ending with a P row*.

CHART FOR TRACKS

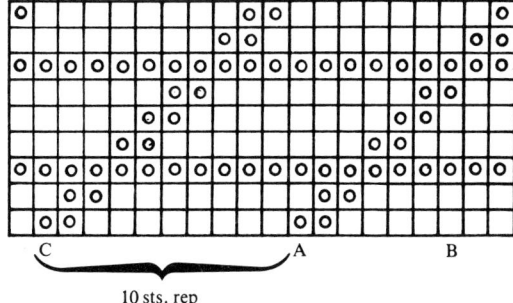

C   A   B

10 sts. rep

St. marked A = beg. of K row for 1st and 3rd sizes, then rep. 10 sts. marked to end
St. marked B = beg. of K row for 2nd and 4th sizes, then rep. 10 sts. marked to end
St. marked C = beg. of P rows for all sizes

O brown yarn
All rem. squares are grey yarn

To shape raglan:
1st row: K1,K2togtbl, K to last 3, K2tog., K1.
2nd row: P.
Repeat these two rows until 21(21 23 25) sts rem., ending with the P row.
Leave these sts on a holder.

Front

Work as for back as far as*.
Dec. the raglan in the same way as for the back until 33(35 39 41) sts rem., ending with a P row.

To shape neck:
Next row: K1, K2togtbl, K8(9 10 10), turn and complete this side first.
**Continue to dec. raglan as before on armhole edge only on every alt. row; at the same time, dec. 1 st. at neck edge on next 5 rows.
Keeping neck edge straight, continue to dec. at raglan edge only as before until 2 sts rem.
Next row: K2tog. Fasten off**.

Place centre 11(11 13 15) sts on a holder. Rejoin yarn to rem. sts and repeat from ** to **.

Sleeves

Both alike, in blue yarn throughout.
Using smaller needles, cast on 33(33 37 37) sts.
Work 2in (5cm) in K1P1 rib as given for back.

Change to larger needles and st.st.
Inc. 1 st. each end of every 5th row to 53(59 63 67) sts.
Work straight to a total measurement of 12½(13½ 15 16½)in, 32(34 38 42)cm, or required length, ending with a P row.

To shape raglan:
Dec. 1 st. each end of every other row, as given for the raglan shaping on back, until 21(21 25 25) sts rem., ending with a P row.
Next row: K1,K2togtbl, K to last 3, K2tog., K1.
Next row: K1,P2tog., P to last 3, P2togtbl, K1.
Repeat these 2 rows until 5 sts rem.
Leave these sts on a holder.

Neckband

Do not press. Using backstitch, carefully join both front and left back raglan seams. Using smaller needles, and blue yarn, with right side of work facing, pick up and K the

21(21 23 25) sts from the back neck holder, working 2tog. in the centre; 5 sts from the top of the left sleeve; 8(8 9 9) sts down the left front neck slope; the 11(11 13 15) sts from the front neck holder; 8(8 9 9) sts up the right front neck slope; and 5 sts from the top of the right sleeve: 57(57 63 67) sts.
Work 2½in (6cm) in K1P1 rib as given for back.
Cast off loosely in rib.

Tunnel

This is worked upside down, in st.st., on larger needles in green yarn.
Cast on 21(21 24 24) sts.
Next row: P.
Inc. 1 st. at beg. of every K row until there are 29(29 32 32) sts.
Next row: P.
Next row: inc. 1 st. in first st., K7, turn and P back.
Continue on these 9 sts:
1st row: inc. 1 st. in first st., K to last 2, K2togtbl.
2nd row: P.
Rep. these 2 rows 3 times.
Cast off.

Rejoin yarn to rem. sts.
Cast off 4(4 5 5), K to end.
1st row: P to last 2 sts, P2tog.
2nd row: K2tog., K to end.
Rep. these 2 rows.
Next row: P to last 2 sts, P2tog.
Work straight on the rem. 12(12 14 14) sts until work measures 8in (20cm) from the cast on edge.
Cast off.

Tunnel edge

Using smaller needles and brown yarn, and with right side facing, pick up and K38 sts around the whole inside edge of the tunnel piece. Work 1in (2½cm) in K1P1 rib.
Cast off in rib.

TRAIN

Main piece
In red yarn, cast on 19 sts.
Work 5in (13cm) straight.
Cast off.

Funnel

In red yarn, cast on 8 sts.
Work 3in (8cm) straight.
Cast off.

Cab

In red yarn, cast on 12 sts.
Work 4in (10cm) straight.
Cast off.

Making up

Do not press. Make up the jumper matching all colours and pattern. Turn neckband on to wrong side and loosely slip st. down. Attach tunnel immediately above welt and catch down along bottom edge, up the side seam, over the top and immediately above the grey stripe. Double the main piece of the train, seam and lightly stuff. Double the cab and tunnel, seam, lightly stuff and attach open ended to the top of the engine.

Embroider wheels and stripes in black and yellow double knitting yarns. Embroider cloud shapes in white double knitting yarn.

92

SEASCAPE

This is the only jumper I have ever seen that lights up! Great fun for darker evenings and reading in bed, as well as for genuine seaside explorations. This modern use of a traditional stitch pattern immediately suggests waves, especially in sea green yarn and blue yarn, and a lighthouse, boat and a mermaid are essential seaside accessories. (Pictures p. 95 and p. 96)

Sizes
To fit chest up to 26(up to 30)in, up to 61(up to 76)cm.

Materials
In Wendy Shetland double knitting:
4(5) × 50gm balls of blue yarn; 3(4) × 50gm, balls of turquoise yarn; 1(1) × 50gm ball of brown yarn. Small quantity of white and flesh pink double knitting yarns. Small quantity of metallic yarn. Small quantity of washable toy stuffing. One pencil torch.
Circular needles are required in the main size and 2 sizes smaller for the main body of the garment.

Tension
24 sts and 32 rows = 4in (10cm) on size 8 (4mm) needles in st.st.

Special abbreviation
M1 = make 1 by lifting the loop between the needle points and knitting into the back of it.

TO KNIT BASIC JUMPER

Sleeves and shoulder yoke
Worked all in one piece, in blue yarn, from one side to the other.
Using needles 2 sizes smaller than those chosen for main tension, e.g. size 10 (3¼mm), cast on 44(46) sts.

Work 2in (5cm) in K1P1 rib.

Change to larger needles, e.g. size 8 (4mm), and cont. in rib.
Next row: inc. 1 st. in every st.: 88(92) sts.
Cont. in K1P1 rib, inc. 1 st. each end of every 9th(7th) row until there are 104(120) sts, working all increases into the rib, and keeping rib correct.
Cont. in rib until work measures 12½(15)in, 32(38)cm.
Mark this point.
Cont. in rib for a further 3½(4)in, 9(10)cm straight.

To divide for neck:
Next row: Rib 52(60) sts, turn.
Rib 7(8)in, 18(20)cm on these sts only, ending at inside edge.
Break off yarn.

Rejoin yarn to rem. sts.
Rib 7(8)in, 18(20)cm on these sts, ending at outside edge.
Rib across all 104(120) sts and work a further 3½(4)in, 9(10)cm straight.
Mark this point.
Measure the distance on the first sleeve between the end of the increasing and the first marked point. Work this same distance straight from the second marked point.
Keeping rib correct and working all decreases into the rib, dec. 1 st. each end of next, then every foll. 9th(7th) row until there are 88(92) sts.
Rib 8(6) rows.
Next row: (work 2tog.) to end: 44(46) sts.

Change to smaller needles.
Work 2in (5cm) in K1P1 rib.
Cast off loosely in rib.

Back and front

Worked all in one piece upside down from
yoke.

Double sleeves and shoulder yoke with neck slit
at the top, and, matching all shapings, carefully
join underarm seams from cuff to marked point
at each side.

Do not press.

Using a circular needle of the size chosen for the
main tension and turquoise yarn, beg. at one
underarm, pick up and K, with right side facing,
at the rate of 8 sts per 1in (2½cm), 110(132) sts
across the bottom edge of one side of the yoke
to the other underarm and 110(132) sts back
across the other side: 220(264) sts.

Clearly mark this point, which is the beg. of a
round.

Work the wave pattern:
1st to 6th rounds: P.
7th round: **K2tog., K3,M1,K1,M1,K3,
K2togtbl,** rep. from ** to ** to end of round.
8th round: K.
Rep. 7th and 8th rounds twice.
These 12 rounds complete the pattern.
Repeat the 12 pattern rounds until turquoise
wave section measures 7½(9½)in, 19(24)cm,
ending with 6th round.

For smaller size only:

Next round: (K1[K2tog., K2] 27 times, K1)
twice: (166 sts).
Change to brown yarn and use a circular needle
two sizes smaller than that chosen for main
tension.
Next round: K113, place the last 20 sts just
worked on to a holder, K43, place the last 20 sts
just worked on to a holder, K rem. 10 sts of the
round.
Next round: K1,(P1,K1) to before the first
holder, cast on 20 sts, (P1,K1) to 1 st. before
2nd holder, P1, cast on 20 sts, (K1,P1) to end of
round.

For larger size only:

Next round: (K11[K2tog., K1] 37 times, K10)
twice: (190 sts).
Change to brown yarn and smaller needle.
Next round: K131, place the last 20 sts just
worked on to a holder, K43, place the last 20 sts

just worked on to a holder, K rem. 16 sts of
round.
Next round: K1,(P1,K1) to before first holder,
cast on 20 sts, (P1,K1) to 1 st. before 2nd
holder, P1, cast on 20 sts, (K1,P1) to end of
round.

For both sizes:

Cont. in rounds of K1,P1 rib until a total of
3in (8cm) has been worked, ending after a
complete round.
Cast off loosely in rib.

Pockets

For each pocket:

At back of work, pick up and K1,P1 rib, using
smaller needles and brown yarn, 20 sts from the
holder.
Work a total of 2¾in (7cm) in rib.
Cast off loosely in rib.

Making up

Do not press. As invisibly as possible catch the
pockets down on to the wrong side of the front
welt.

MERMAID

Body

Using pink yarn and larger needles, cast on
8 sts.
Next row: P.
Next row: inc. 1 st. in every st. in K: (16 sts).
Work in st.st. to a total length of 2in (5cm).

Work 2 rows of blue and blue metallic yarn,
used together.
Work 2 rows of turquoise and green metallic
yarn.
Cont. working in 2-row stripes of blue/blue
metallic yarn and turquoise/green metallic yarn
for 3in (8cm), ending after a complete stripe.
Cast off.

Arms

Using main needles and pink yarn, cast on 2 sts.
Next row: P.
Cont. in st.st. beg. K and inc. 1 st. each end of
next then every alt. row to 6 sts.
Work 7 rows straight.
Next row: K2tog. to end.

Run a thread through rem. sts and use to seam arm.

Making up
Fold mermaid into a tube, gather the pink cast on edge firmly and seam. Stuff. Fold the blue end flat with the seam central at the back and close. Gather a 'neck' and 'tail', stitching a fin shape into the tail. Embroider features and add yellow hair. Stuff arms and attach.

LIGHTHOUSE

Using main needles in white yarn, cast on 12 sts.
Work straight in st.st. to a total length of
4½in (11cm).
Cast off.

Making up
Seam the lighthouse into a tube and close the bottom and stuff the bottom only. Insert the torch in the top. Embroider the door, steps and windows in black yarn. Leave the top open for easy removal of torch for washing and battery changes. Embroider turquoise and white waves around the 'rock' pockets.

BOAT

Sails
Cast on 30 sts on main needles in white.
1st row: K.
Next row: K2tog., K to last 2, K2togtbl.
Rep. the last 2 rows until 2 sts rem.
K2tog., fasten off.

Boat
Cast on 20 sts on main needles in red.
1st row: K.
Inc. 1 st. each end of every row to 26 sts.
Cast off.

Pennant
Cast on 7 sts on main needles in red.
Rep. the 2 rows as given for the sail until 3 sts rem.
K3tog., fasten off.

Stitch the boat on above the 'horizon', embroidering a red mast in chain st.

ELECTRIC

A must for the arcade or computer game addict, this jacket is embroidered in the brightest colours possible on a dark background; it is nearly as dazzling and compulsive as the real thing.

Embroider any figures that your family's game buff is into, but most are based on lines and little figures. You can, of course, be as ambitious as you like – good luck with 'the Hobbit' or 'Elite'. (Picture p. 98)

Sizes
To fit chest 24(26 28 30)in, 61(66 71 76)cm.

Materials
In Patons Beehive double knitting 6(6 6 6) × 50gm balls of navy yarn. Scraps of neon and other bright coloured yarns. Zip fastener. Clip on stars and studs as required.

Tension
24 sts and 32 rows = 4in (10cm) on size 8 (4mm) needles in st.st.

Back
With needles 2 sizes smaller than those chosen for main tension, e.g. size 10 (3¼mm), cast on 78(84 90 96) sts.
Work 20 rows in K1,P1 rib.

Change to needles chosen for main tension, e.g. size 8 (4mm), and st.st.
Work straight until work measures 16(16½ 18½ 19½)in, 41(42 47 50)cm, ending with a P row.
Cast off 28(30 33 33) sts at beg. of next 2 rows.
Leave rem. 22(24 24 30) sts on a holder for back neck.

Left front
Using smaller needles, cast on 40(42 44 48) sts.

Work 20 rows in K1,P1 rib.

Change to larger needles and work straight in st.st. until work measures 16(16 20 20) rows shorter than the back, ending with a P row**.
Work 1 row so ending at neck edge.

To shape neck:
Next row: cast off 6(6 6 8) sts at beg. of row (neck edge).
Dec. 1 st. at neck edge on next 3(3 3 4) rows.
Dec. 1 st. at neck edge on every alt. row until 28(30 33 33) sts rem.
Work straight until front measures the same as back to shoulder.
Cast off.

Right front
Work as given for left front as far as **.

To shape neck:
Work as given for left front.

Sleeves
Make 2, both alike.
Using smaller needles, cast on 43(43 45 45) sts.
1st row: (K1,P1) rep. to last st., K1.
2nd row: K1,(K1,P1) rep. to last 2 sts, K2.
Rep. these 2 rows until 20 rows of rib have been worked.

Change to larger needles and st.st.
Inc. 1 st. each end of 3rd, then every foll. 5th(5th 5th 5th) row until there are 73(73 79 85) sts.
Work straight to a total length of 12½(13½ 15 17½)in, 32(34 38 44)cm.
Cast off loosely.

Neckband
Carefully join both shoulder seams.

Using smaller needles, pick up and K, with right side facing, 6(6 6 8) sts across top of right front neck; 12(12 15 15) sts up right front slope, K22(24 24 30) sts from back neck holder; 12(12 15 15) sts down left front slope; 6(6 6 8) sts across top of left front neck: 58(60 66 76) sts.

Next row: K1,P1 rib to st. before centre neck, rib 2tog., rib to end, ending K1.

1st row: (K1,P1) rep. to last st., K1.

2nd row: K1,(K1,P1) rep. to last 2 sts, K2.

Rep. these 2 rows until 10 rows of rib have been worked.

To shape the collar:
Change to needles one size larger, e.g. size 9 (3¾mm).

Work 10(10 10 10) rows in rib.

Change to needles one size larger again, e.g. size 8 (4mm).

Work 10(10 10 10) rows in rib.

Cast off loosely in rib.

Making up
Do not press. Make up rem. seams and insert zip. Embroider chosen games motifs in bright colours. Add stars and studs if wished.

DRESS AND DUNGAREES

Sizes
To fit chest 18(20)in, 46(51)cm.

Materials
In Wendy Family Choice double knitting, small quantities of red, orange, yellow, green, blue, royal blue and lilac yarns. 4 large press fasteners. 7in (18cm) of elastic (optional).

Tension
24 sts and 32 rows = 4in (10cm) on size 8 (4mm) needles in st.st.

Stripe pattern
Work the foll. 6-row stripe pattern throughout both garments, in the foll. order of yarns.
6 rows lilac
6 rows royal blue
6 rows blue
6 rows green
6 rows yellow
6 rows orange
6 rows red.

DRESS

Back
Using needles chosen for main tension, e.g. size 8 (4mm), and lilac yarn, cast on 114(122) sts. Work 4 rows in K.

Change to st.st., starting K row, and cont. colour sequence by working 2 more lilac rows, then 6 rows royal blue.
Cont. in st.st. in 6-row stripes of yarn colour sequence until work measures 8in (20cm), ending with the 4th row of the colour being used.

Change to needles 2 sizes smaller than those chosen for main tension, e.g. size 10 (3¼mm),

and keep colour sequence correct.
Next row: (K2tog.) to end: 57(61) sts.
Next row: K1,(P1,K1) to end.

Change to next yarn colour and cont. in rib, working first and last st. of every row in K, and keeping rib correct in between, continuing in colour sequence.
Cast off loosely in rib in the colour in which the last rib row was worked.

Front
Work as given for back as far as * matching colours throughout.
Using colour in which the last rib row was worked, cast off 12 sts loosely in rib, rib to last 12 sts, cast off these 12 sts loosely in rib.

Rejoin yarn for next colour to rem. sts and change to larger needles.
Keeping rib correct in the same way as before, and cont. to keep colour sequence correct, work approx. 4½in (11cm), ending with the 5th row of a colour stripe.
Next row: rib 7, and leave this colour attached.
** Change colour and work 8½in (22cm) in colour sequence on these 7 sts.
Cast off **.

Beg. where colour at end of bib piece was left and using this colour, cast off in rib to last 7 sts, rib 7.
Work as given for other strap from ** to **.

DUNGAREES

Back
To make leg:
Keep stripe colour sequence correct throughout.

Using smaller needles and lilac yarn, cast on 25 sts.
1st row: *K1,P1, rep. from* to last st., K1.
2nd row: *P1,K1, rep. from* to last st., P1.
Rep. these 2 rows until rib measures 1in (2½cm), ending with a 1st row.
Next row: rib 6, *rib and inc. into next st., rep. from* 12 times, rib. rem. 7 sts: 37 sts.

Change to larger needles and starting with a K row, work straight in st.st. until leg measures 9in (24cm) from start of st.st., ending with a P row.
1st row: cast off 2 sts at beg. of row.
2nd row: P.
3rd row: cast off 2 sts at beg. of row.
4th row: P.
5th row: dec. 1 st. at beg. of row.
6th row: P.
7th row: dec. 1 st. at beg. of row.
Leave rem. 31 sts on a spare needle.

Work a further leg piece to match, reversing all shapings.

To make body:
Keep stripe colour sequence correct throughout.
**Next row: with wrong side facing, P across sts of first leg piece, then P across sts of second leg piece: 62 sts.
Work straight on these sts until back measures 17in (43cm) from start of st.st., ending with a P row**.

To shape back:
Next row: work to last 8 sts, turn.
Rep. this row once.
Next row: work to last 16 sts, turn.
Rep. this row once.
Next row: work to last 24 sts, turn.
Next row: work to last 24 sts, then break yarn and rejoin to beg. of row.
***Work 1 row in K across all sts.

Change to smaller needles and, starting with a 2nd row, work in rib as for ankle rib, dec. 1 st. at beg. of 1st row only (61 sts).
Cont. to rib for 1½in (4cm), ending with a 2nd row***.
Cast off in rib.

Front
To make leg:
Keep stripe colour sequence correct throughout.
Using smaller needles and lilac yarn cast on 25 sts.
Work in rib as given for the ankle rib on back leg for 1in (2½cm), ending with a 1st row.
Next row: rib 5, *rib and inc. into next st., rib 1, rep. from* 8 times, rib rem. 4 sts: 33 sts.

Change to larger needles and, starting with a K row, work straight in st.st. until leg measures 9in (24cm) from start of st.st., ending with a P row.
Next row: dec. 1 st at beg. of row.
Next row: P.
Next row: dec. 1 st. at beg. of row.
Leave rem. 31 sts. on a spare needle.

Work a further leg piece to match, reversing all shapings.

To make body:
Work as given for back from **to**.
Then work as given for back from ***to***.
Work as given for dress front from *to end.

Making up
Do not press. Join all seams, carefully matching colour stripes and, if preferred, doubling the back waist welt on to the wrong side and loosely slip stitching it down to form an elastic casing. Trim elastic to chosen length, insert and firmly secure at each end. Attach large press fasteners to fasten straps, crossed at back waist.

PARTY DRESS

Sizes
To fit chest 18(20)in, 46(51)cm.

Materials
In Wendy Family Choice double knitting, 2 × 50gm balls of white yarn. Scraps of lilac, dark blue, light blue, green, yellow, orange and red yarns. 1 white and 4 coloured buttons.

Tension
24 sts and 32 rows = 4in (10cm) on size 8 (4mm) needles in st.st.

Main piece

Using needles chosen for main tension, e.g. size 8 (4mm), and lilac yarn, cast on 192(198) sts. Work 1 row in K.
* Work 2 rows each in K of every colour yarn, in the foll. sequence:
dark blue, light blue, green, yellow, orange and red * .

Change to white yarn and st.st.
Starting with a K row, work straight to a total length of 10(11)in, 25(28)cm, ending with a P row.
Next row: (K2tog., K1) 24(27) times, (K2tog.) 24(18) times, (K2tog., K1) 24(27) times: 120(126) sts.
1st row: K1,(P1,K2) to last.2 sts, P1,K1.
2nd row: K1,(K1,P2) to last 2, K2.
Keep this rib correct in this way, by rep. these 2 rows, throughout the rem. of the work, always working the 2 sts at the extreme edges in K.
Rib 2in (5cm) straight, ending with a wrong side row.

To divide for armholes:
Next row: cast on 2 sts, K these 2 sts and the next st., rib 23(24), turn.

⁑Work straight on these 26(27) sts in rib, keeping 3 sts in K at outside edge, until 4½(5)in 11(13)cm have been worked on these sts, ending at inside (armhole) edge.
Next row: cast off 11(13) sts, work to end and place the rem. 15(14) sts on to a holder⁑.

Rejoin yarn to rem. sts, cast off 12 sts, and rib until 48(52) sts have been worked, turn.
Work 3¾(4½)in, 9½(11)cm on these sts in rib.

To shape neck:
Next row: rib 17(19) sts, turn, work 2tog., rib to end.
**Keeping rib correct, dec. 1 st. at neck edge of next 5 rows: 11(13) sts.
Work 1 row in rib.
Cast off**.
Place centre 14 sts on to a holder.

Rejoin yarn to neck edge of rem. sts, work 2tog., work to end.
Rep. from ** to **.

Rejoin yarn to rem. sts, cast off 12 sts and rib to end.
Next row: cast on 2 sts, K these 2 sts and the next st., rib to end.
Work as given for the other side from ⁑ to ⁑, at the same time, after 3 rows have been worked, make a buttonhole.

To make a buttonhole:
Next row: K1,K2tog, yon, rib to end.
Make 3 further buttonholes in the same way in the garter st. edge at approx. 1in (2½cm) intervals.

Sleeves
Make 2, both alike.
Using needles one size smaller than those

chosen for main tension, e.g. size 9 (3¾mm), and lilac yarn, cast on 54 sts.
Work 1 row in K.
Work as given for main piece from * to *.

Change to larger needles and white yarn.
Next row: K.
Next row: (P1, inc. 1 st. in next st. in P) to end: 81 sts.
Work straight in st.st. to a total of 1½(1¾)in 4(4½)cm, ending with a P row.
Mark this row.
Work 5 more rows.
Next row: (K1,K2tog.) to end: 54 sts.
Next row: P.
Cast off.

Neckband
Join both shoulder seams in back stitch.

Using one size smaller needles and white yarn, and with right side facing, pick up and K15(14) sts from left back neck; 6 sts down left front neck slope; 14 sts from holder at front neck; 6 sts up right front neck slope; 15(14) sts from right back neck.
Work 5 rows in K, working a buttonhole, as given for main piece, in the 3rd row.
Cast off.

Making up
Do not press. Seam sleeves from cuff end to marked row. Ease the rem. of the top sleeve edges into the armhole, with the sleeve seam above the centre underarm point. Join centre back seam up to the same height as the division for the armholes. Add the buttons to match the buttonholes.

DECK CHAIR

This cool cotton shift is the ideal beach cover up for burnt knees, and the top, or the sleeves added to the dress, do the same for roasted shoulders. Each garment is made from diagonally knitted striped squares in deck chair colours, the sleeves being half squares. To make a bigger version, perhaps for yourself, just keep knitting until the edge measurement of your square is the width required for your size, then dec. down to nothing. (Picture opposite)

Sizes
To fit chest 24(26 28 30)in, 61(66 71 76)cm.

Materials
For the dress, in Patons Cotton Perle:
2(3 3 4) × 50gm balls of cream yarn;
1(1 2 2) × 50gm balls of green yarn;
1(1 1 1) × 50gm ball of blue yarn;
1(1 1 1) × 50gm ball of pink yarn.
3.3yd/3m of ribbon.

For the top, in Patons Cotton Perle:
2(2 3 3) × 50gm balls of cream yarn;
1(1 1 2) × 50gm balls of green yarn;
1(1 1 1) × 50gm ball of blue yarn;
1(1 1 1) × 50gm ball of pink yarn.
3.3yd/3m of ribbon.

Tension
22 sts and 29 rows = 4in (10cm) on size 8 (4mm) needles in st.st.

Stripe pattern
All pieces are worked in the following striped pattern in st.st. kept correct throughout:
6 rows cream
2 rows blue
2 rows cream
2 rows blue
6 rows cream
4 rows green
4 rows pink
4 rows green
These 30 rows are repeated throughout.

Main piece
Make 2 for the top, 4 for the dress.
Using needles chosen for main tension, e.g. size 8 (4mm), cast on 2 sts in cream yarn.
Work in st.st. and stripe pattern as given.
1st row: K, inc. 1 st. at each end.
2nd row: P, inc. 1 st. at beg. only.
3rd row: K, inc. 1 st. at each end.
4th row: P, inc. 1 st. at end only.
Cont. to inc. in this way, by rep. these 4 rows, and keeping the stripe pattern correct, until the edges of the work (not the work measured straight) each measure 13(14 15 16)in, 33(36 38 41)cm, ending with a K row*.
Next row: P, without shaping.
1st row: K2tog., K to last 2 sts, K2togtbl.
2nd row: P2togtbl, P to end.
3rd row: K2tog, K to last 2 sts, K2togtbl.
4th row: P to last 2 sts, P2tog.
Cont. to dec. in this way, by rep. 1st to 4th row, keeping stripe pattern correct until 2 sts rem.
Work 2tog., fasten off.

Sleeves
Make 2, both alike.
Work as given for main pieces as far as *.
Cast off loosely.

Making up
Seam the pieces, matching the stripes and leaving 7(7 8 8)in, 18(18 20 20)cm, armholes and a 10in (25cm) neck opening. Leave 7in (18)cm slits up the side seams of the dress. The sleeves are attached centrally at the shoulder edge by their longest sides. Stitch ribbon on to the right side around all the edges, mitring the corners where necessary.

CHERRY-RIPE

This little jumper is scattered with bobbles worked in red yarn and these are turned into cherries with embroidered stems. However, the bobbles could be anything: work them in yellow yarn and embroider petals around them; or in blue yarn with a smile under each resulting pair of eyes; or even in multi-colours with no embroidery at all. (Picture p. 110)

Sizes
To fit chest 20(22 24)in, 51(56 61)cm.

Materials
In Patons Clansman double knitting:
5(5 6) × 50gm balls of cream yarn; 1 × 50gm ball of dark red yarn. Scraps of green yarn. 2 buttons.

Tension
24 sts and 32 rows = 4in (10cm) on size 8 (4mm) needles in st.st.

To make a bobble
Work in red yarn.
Twist the red yarn around the background cream yarn.
Next row: K into the front, the back, the front, and the back of the same st., turn.
Working these 4 sts. only, P, turn, K, turn, P, turn, K all 4 sts together.
Twist the red yarn once around the background cream yarn after making the bobble to make it firmer.
Tie the two red ends together and cut leaving 1in (2½cm) ends.

Back
Using needles 2 sizes smaller than those chosen for main tension, e.g. size 10 (3¼mm), and cream yarn, cast on 67(73 79) sts.
1st row: (K1,P1) rep. to last st., K1.

2nd row: K1,(K1,P1) rep. to last 2 sts, K2.
Rep. these 2 rows until 2in (5cm) have been worked, and working 2tog. at the end of the last row: 66(72 78) sts.

Change to larger needles, e.g. size 8 (4mm), st.st. and pattern.
1st to 14th row: st.st., beg. K.
15th row: K7(10 13) in cream yarn, [make bobble in red yarn in next st., K6 in cream yarn, make bobble in red yarn in next st., K14 in cream yarn] twice, make bobble in red yarn in next st., K6 in cream yarn, make bobble in red yarn in next st., K7(10 13) in cream yarn.
16th to 30th row: st.st., starting P.
31st row: K3(6 9) in cream yarn, make bobble in next st. in red yarn, [K14 in cream yarn, make bobble in next st. in red yarn, K6 in cream yarn, make bobble in next st. in red yarn] twice, K14 in cream yarn, make bobble in next st. in red yarn, K3(6 9) in cream yarn.
32nd row: P.
These 32 rows form the pattern and are rep. throughout the work. When shaping occurs, keep cherries in the same places, above one another, as before, omitting any that occur one or two sts. from the edge of the work.
Work straight to a total of 10½(11½ 12½)in, 27(28 32)cm, or required length, ending with a P row*.

To shape armholes:
Cast off 3 sts at beg. of next 2 rows.
Dec. 1 st. each end of every alt. row to 54(58 62) sts.
Work straight until armholes measure 4½(5 5½)in, 11(13 14)cm, ending at least 2 rows after a bobble row.

To shape shoulders:
Cast off 7(7 8) sts at beg. of next 2 rows.

Cast off 7(8 8) sts at beg. of foll. 2 rows.
Leave rem. 26(28 30) sts on a holder.

Front

Work as given for back as far as *.

To shape armholes and divide for neck:

Cast off 3 sts at beg. of next 2 rows.
Next row: K2togtbl, K to last 2, K2tog.
Next row: P31(34 37), turn.
Work on these sts only.
1st row: K to last 2, K2tog.
2nd row: P to last 4, K4.
Rep. the last 2 rows 1(2 3) times.

To make buttonhole:

Next row: K2, yon, K2tog., K to end.
Keeping 4 sts in K at neck edge on every row,
work straight until armhole measures
3¾(4 4)in, 9½(10 10)cm, making a second
buttonhole on the foll. 12th row and finishing at
the neck edge.

To shape neck:

Work 8(9 10) sts at beg of next row, and place
the sts just worked on a holder, then dec. 1 st. at
neck edge of every row to 14(15 16) sts.
If necessary work straight until armhole
measures same as on back, ending at armhole
edge.
Cast off 7(7 8) sts at beg of next row.
Work 1 row.
Cast off.

Rejoin yarn to rem. sts at neck edge and cast on
4 sts at beg. (neck edge) of row.
Keeping these sts in K throughout, work this
side to match the first, omitting buttonholes and
reversing all shapings, i.e. working armhole
dec. as K2togtbl, at row beginnings.

Sleeves

Make 2, in cream yarn, both alike.
Cast on 43(45 47) sts on smaller needles.
Work 2in (5cm) in K1,P1 rib as given for back,
working 2tog. at end of last row: 42(44 46) sts.

Change to st.st. and work 14 rows starting with
K.

Next row: K7(8 9) in cream yarn, make bobble
in next st. in red yarn, K6 in cream yarn, make
bobble in next st. in red yarn, K14 in cream
yarn, make bobble in next st. in red yarn, K6 in
cream yarn, make bobble in next st. in red yarn,
K7(8 9) in cream yarn.
Cont. in the same way as given for back, making
bobbles on the 31st row alternate with those on
the 15th row, at the same time, inc. 1 st. each
end of 9th and every foll. 8th row to
56(60 64) sts.
Work straight to a total length of
10(10½ 11)in, 25(27 28)cm, or required length
to underarm, ending with a P row.

To shape top:

Cast off 3 sts at beg. of next 2 rows.
Dec. 1 st. each end of every alt. row to
44(46 48) sts.
Cast off 3 sts at beg. of next 10 rows.
Cast off rem. 14(16 18) sts.

Collar

Work in cream yarn without bobbles.
Carefully join both shoulder seams in back
stitch. With right side facing, in cream yarn and
using smaller needles, K sts from holder at right
front neck; pick up and K evenly 12(12 12) sts
up right front neck; 26(28 30) sts from holder at
back neck, working 2tog. at centre;
12(12 12) sts evenly down left front neck; sts
from rem. holder: 65(69 73) sts.
1st row: K4,(K1,P1) to last 5 sts, K5.
2nd row: K4,(P1,K1) to last 5 sts, P1,K4.
Rep. these 2 rows 6 times.

Change to needles 1 size larger, e.g. size
9 (3¾mm), and rep. 1st and 2nd rows twice.

Change to needles 1 size larger again, e.g. size
8 (4mm), and rep. 1st and 2nd rows twice.
Cast off loosely in rib.

Making up

Do not press. Make up all rem. seams carefully
in back stitch, aligning all bobble rows where
possible. Embroider green stems in stem stitch;
attach buttons.

110

TREE

Children love being in trees. With this jumper they can be in a tree, quite safely, in the most unlikely places, such as in the supermarket queue, or in the car. The apples on the tree could easily be birds, flowers, cherries, squirrels, Christmas tree decorations, caterpillars, owls or any or everything that spends time up a tree. (Picture p. 111)

Sizes
To fit chest 24–26(28–30)in, 61–66(71–76)cm.

Materials
In Jaeger Naturgarn Lopi: 3(4) × 100gm balls of blue yarn; 2(3) × 100gm balls of light green yarn; 1(1) × 100gm ball of dark green yarn; 1(1) × 100gm ball of mid-brown yarn. 5 brown buttons. Approximately 20 apple buttons.

Tension
16 sts and 20 rows = 4in (10cm) on size 4 (6mm) needles in st.st.

Back
Using needles 2 sizes smaller than those chosen for main tension, e.g. size 6 (5mm), and dark green yarn, cast on 56(64) sts and work 2in (5cm) in K2P2 rib.

Change to larger needles, e.g. size 4 (6mm), and st.st.
Work 1½in (4cm) in dark green yarn, ending with a P row.

Change to blue yarn.
Work to a total length of 9½(11½)in, 24(29)cm, ending with a P row.
Work the foll. 6 rows to change from blue yarn to light green yarn.
1st row: (K3 blue, 2 light green, 3 blue) rep. to end.

2nd row: (P3 blue, 2 light green, 3 blue) rep. to end.
3rd row: (K2 blue, 4 light green, 2 blue) rep. to end.
4th row: (P2 blue, 4 light green, 2 blue) rep. to end.
5th row: (K1 blue, 6 light green, 1 blue) rep. to end.
6th row: (P1 blue, 6 light green, 1 blue) rep. to end.
Cont. in light green yarn to a total measurement of 17½(20½)in, 44(52)cm, ending with a P row.
Cast off 18(21) sts, K until 18(21) sts rem., place the 20(22) sts just worked on to a holder, cast off rem. 18(21) sts.

Right front
Using smaller needles and dark green yarn, cast on 24(28) sts.
Work 2in (5cm) in K2P2 rib.

Change to larger needles and st.st.
Work 1½in (4cm) in dark green yarn, ending with a P row.

Change to blue yarn.
Work to a total length of 9½(11½)in, 24(29)cm, ending with a P row.
Work the foll. 6 rows to change from blue yarn to light green yarn.

On the smaller size only:
Work 1st–6th rows of pattern change as given for back.

On the larger size only:
1st row: (K3 blue, 2 light green, 3 blue) rep. to last 4, K3 blue, 1 light green.
2nd row: P1 light green, 3 blue, (3 blue, 2 light green, 3 blue) rep. to end.
3rd row: (K2 blue, 4 light green, 2 blue) rep. to

last 4, K2 blue, 2 light green.
4th row: P2 light green, 2 blue, (2 blue, 4 light green, 2 blue) rep. to end.
5th row: (K1 blue, 6 light green, 1 blue) rep. to last 4, K1 blue, 3 light green.
6th row: P3 light green, 1 blue (1 blue, 6 light green, 1 blue) rep. to end*.

To shape neck:
Cont. in plain light green yarn.
Next row: K2tog, K to end.
Cont. to keep armhole edge straight, dec. 1 st. at same neck edge on every 3rd row until 18(21) sts rem. **
Work straight until total side edge matches that on back.
Cast off.

Left front
Work as given for right front as far as *.

To shape neck:
Cont. in plain light green.
Next row: K to last 2 sts, K2togtbl.
Cont. to keep armhole edge straight, dec. 1 st. at same neck edge on every 3rd row until 18(21) sts rem.
Work as given for right front from **.

Sleeves
Make 2, both alike.
Using smaller needles and dark green yarn, cast on 30(30) sts.
Work 2in (5cm) in K2P2 rib.

Change to larger needles and st.st.
Work 1½in (4cm) ending with a P row; at the same time begin to inc. 1 st. each end of every 3rd row.

Change to blue yarn.
Cont. to inc. in the same way until there are 56(64) sts.
Work straight to a total measurement of 11½(14½)in, 29(37)cm, ending with a P row.
Work the 6 colour change rows from blue yarn to light green yarn as given for back.
Next row: K.
Cast off loosely.

Collar/button band
Carefully join both shoulder seams in self colour.
Using smaller needles and mid-brown yarn, with right side facing, pick up and K, at the rate of 4 sts per 1in (2½cm), 42(50) sts up the right front side to beg. of neck shaping, including the welt; 30 sts up the right neck slope; 20(22) sts from the back neck holder, working 2tog. in the centre; 30 sts down the left front slope; 42(50) sts down the whole of rem. front edge: 163(181) sts.
1st row: (K1,P1) rep. to last st., K1.
2nd row: K1,(K1,P1) rep. to last 2 sts, K2.
Rep. these 2 rows until 1in (2½cm) has been worked ending at the bottom of the edge at which you wish to make the buttonholes.
Next row: rib 4, *** work 2tog., yon, rib 7(9) ***, rep. from *** to *** 3 times, work 2tog., yon, rib to end.
Next row: rib, working all sts into the rib pattern.
Work until 2in (5cm) of rib has been completed.

To shape collar:
Cast off, in rib, 57(65) sts at beg. of next 2 rows: 49(51) sts.

Change to needles one size larger, e.g. size 5 (5½mm), and light green yarn.
Work 2in, (5cm) in K1,P1 rib as given before.

Change to needles one size larger again, i.e. those chosen for main tension).
Work 6 rows.

Change to needles one size larger again, e.g. size 3 (6½mm).
Work 6 rows.

Cast off loosely in rib.

Making up
Make up rem. seams so that the 7(8)in, 18(20)cm deep armholes begin immediately after the change over from blue yarn to light green yarn. Join all seams matching colour areas and shapings. Stitch on brown buttons to match buttonholes. Stitch apple buttons scattered over the green tree, with some windfalls if preferred.

T-SHIRT

Sizes
To fit chest 18(20)in, 46(51)cm.

Materials
In Wendy Family Choice double knitting, 2 × 50gm balls of white yarn. Scraps of lilac, dark blue, light blue, green, yellow, orange and red yarns.

Tension
24 sts and 32 rows = 4in (10cm) on size 8 (4mm) needles in st.st.

Back and front
Both alike.
Using needles 2 sizes smaller than those chosen for main tension, e.g. size 10(3¼mm), and white yarn, cast on 61(63) sts.
1st row: (K1,P1) rep. to last st., K1.
2nd row: K1,(K1,P1) rep. to last 2 sts, K2.
Rep. these 2 rows 3 times.

Change to larger needles and st.st. and beg. the foll. colour sequence of yarns with a K row:
4 rows white
2 rows lilac
4 rows white
2 rows dark blue
4 rows white
2 rows light blue
4 rows white
2 rows green
4 rows white
2 rows yellow
4 rows white
2 rows orange
4 rows white
2 rows red

These 42 rows are repeated throughout the rem. of the work, including the shoulder rib.
Work straight to a total length of 8(8½)in 20(22)cm, ending after 2 rows of white.

To shape sleeves:
Keeping colour sequence correct, cast on 18(20) sts. at beg. of next 2 rows: 97(103) sts.
Work 4(4½)in, 10(11½)cm straight on these sts, ending with a P row.

To add top shoulder rib:
1st row: K18(20), (K1,P1) to last 19(21) sts, K to end.
2nd row: P18(20), (P1,K1) to last 19(21) sts, P to end.
Rep. these 2 rows once.
Next row: cast off 18(20) sts, keeping rib and st.st. correct as before, work to end.
Next row: cast off 18(20) sts, keeping rib correct, work to end.
Work 3 rows in rib.
Cast off in rib.

Making up
Make up, using back stitch, sleeve top and shoulder seams overlapping the front rib over the back rib and catching down the ends only of the two rib bands as invisibly as possible. The cast off edges of the ribs remain unattached.
Using smaller needles and white yarn, and with right side facing, pick up and K, at the rate of approx. 6 sts per 1in (2½cm), 54(60) sts across the whole of the cuff edge, i.e. 27(30) sts per half.
Work 4 rows in K1,P1 rib.
Cast off in rib.
Carefully join rem. seams.

TRACKSUIT TOP

For someone small and sporting, this 'tracksuit' top will be warm and practical, as well as easy to wash when the halftime oranges get out of hand. Bright colours and white look good, as do mixed pastels, and the badge can, of course, be whatever the owner is keen on. The sleeves are worked in the opposite direction to the usual method, so that the stripes are easy to do and match the shoulder stripes, and the cuffs are picked up and worked afterwards. (Picture p. 118)

Sizes

To fit chest 20(22 24)in, 51(56 61)cm. Sleeve length approx. 11in (28cm).

Materials

In Sirdar Country Style double knitting: 3(3 3) × 50gm balls of blue yarn; 1(1 1) × 50gm ball of white yarn. Stitch-on motif or badge. Open-ended zip fastener.

Tension

24 sts and 32 rows = 4in (10cm) on size 8 (4mm) needles in st.st.

Back

Using needles 2 sizes smaller than those chosen for main tension, e.g. size 10 (3¾mm), and blue yarn, cast on 67(73 79) sts.
1st row: (K1,P1) rep. to last st., K1.
2nd row: K1,(K1,P1) rep. to last 2 sts, K2.
Rep. these 2 rows in the following yarn colour sequence, 6 rows blue, 4 rows white, 6 rows blue.

Change to needles chosen for main tension, e.g. size 8 (4mm) and st.st.
Cont. in blue yarn and work straight to a total length of 13½(14 15)in, 34(36 38)cm.

Change to white yarn.
Work 6 rows.

Change to blue yarn.
Work 2 rows.
Next row: cast off 24(27 29), work to last 24(27 29) and place the 19(19 21) sts just worked on to a holder, cast off rem. sts.

Left front

Using smaller needles and in blue yarn, cast on 33(37 39) sts.
Work in rib as given for back, in the same colour sequence.

Change to larger needles and st.st.
Work in blue yarn until work is 14(14 16) rows shorter than back, ending with a P row*.
Work 1 row in K.
Next row: P4(5 5) and place these sts on to a holder, P2tog., P to end.
**Dec. 1 st. at neck edge on next 4 rows:
Work 1(1 3) rows straight on rem. 24(27 29) sts.

Change to white yarn.
Work 6 rows.

Change to blue yarn.
Work 2 rows.
Cast off.

Right front

Work as given for left front as far as*.
Next row: K4(5 5) and place these sts on to a holder, K2tog., K to end.
Work as given for left front from** to end.

Sleeves

Make 2 both alike, work sideways.
Using larger needles and blue yarn, cast on 12(11 12) sts.

Work 1 row in P.

Working in st.st., starting with a K row, cast on 6(7 7) sts at the beg. of next and every alt. (i.e. every K) row until there are 42(46 54) sts.

Work 18(20 20) rows straight in blue yarn.

Keeping work straight, work 6 rows in white yarn, 2 rows in blue yarn, 6 rows in white yarn and 18(20 20) rows in blue yarn, so ending with a K row.

Work 1 row in P.

Cast off 6(7 7) sts at beg. of next and every alt. (i.e. every K) row until there are 12(11 12) sts.

Work 1 row in P.

Cast off.

Cuffs

Both alike.

Using smaller needles and blue yarn, and with right side facing, pick up and K evenly across the cuff edge 39(41 43) sts (at the rate of approx. 6 sts per 1in (2½cm).

Work in rib as given for back for 16 rows in the same yarn colour sequence. (The sleeve may be lengthened or shortened here by working more or less rib.)

Cast off very loosely in rib.

Neckband

Carefully join both shoulder seams in back stitch.

Using smaller needles and blue yarn, and with right side facing, pick up and K4(5 5) sts from holder at right front neck; 12(12 14) sts up right front slope; 19(19 21) sts from the back neck holder; 12(12 14) sts from the left front slope; and 4(5 5) sts from left front holder: 51(53 59) sts.

Work in rib as given for back, but work 3 rows in blue, 3 rows in white, and 3 rows in blue.

Cast off loosely in rib.

Making up

Do not press. Carefully make up all rem. seams in back stitch, giving armholes 4½(5 5½)in, 11(13 14)cm deep, and carefully matching stripes at the shoulder.

Sew stripes together in self colour. Insert zip and stitch on badge.

BAVARIAN JACKET

Numerous German children still dress like Hansel and Gretel and, whilst not many British youngsters would give you a 'thank you' for lederhosen, they should like this little teutonic jacket. Like the people who wear the real thing, this jacket is practical, hardwearing and easy to get along with. It is fastened with only a bone button and is designed to be worn open over other clothes. If you prefer, attach a zip to close the front opening. (Picture p. 119)

Sizes
To fit chest 20(22 24)in, 51(56 61)cm.

Materials
In Patons Capstan Aran: 3(4 4) × 50gm balls of cream yarn; 1(1 1) × 50gm ball of red yarn; 1(1 1) × 50gm ball of green yarn. 1 bone button.

Tension
19 sts and 25 rows = 4in (10cm) on size 7 (4½mm) needles in st.st.

Main piece
To make border:
With needles 1 size smaller than those chosen for main tension, e.g. size 8 (4mm), and red yarn, cast on 100(110 120) sts.
Work 3 rows in st.st., starting K, and inc. 1 st. each end of every row.

Change to green yarn and cont. to inc. as before until there are 108(118 128) sts.
Still in green yarn and st.st., dec. 1 st. each end of every row until there are 100(110 120) sts, so ending with a P row.

Change to cream yarn.
Work 1 row in K.

Change to needles chosen for main tension, e.g. size 7 (4½mm), and reversed st.st., beg. with K row, and work straight to a length, from the beg. of the cream yarn, of 9½(9½ 10)in, 24(24 25)cm, ending with a K row.

To divide for armholes:
Next row: P19(21 22) sts, turn.
**Work 3(3½ 4)in, 8(9 10)cm on these sts, ending at outside edge (neck edge).

To shape neck:
Work 4(5 5) sts and place these sts on a holder, work to end.
Dec. 1 st. at neck edge on every row until there are 10(11 12) sts.
Work straight until armhole, at armhole edge, measures 4½(5 5½)in, 11(13 14)cm, ending with a K row.
Cast off**.

Rejoin yarn to right-hand edge of rem. sts.
Cast off 11(12 14) sts, P40(44 48), turn.
Work 4½(5 5½)in, 11(13 14)cm straight on these sts, ending with a K row.
Cast off.

Rejoin yarn to right-hand edge of rem. sts.
Cast off 11(12 14) sts, then work as given for first front from ** to **.

Sleeves
Both alike.
Using smaller needles and red yarn, cast on 32(32 34) sts.
Work 3 rows in st.st., starting K.

Change to green yarn, work 5 rows in st.st., ending with a P row.

Change to cream yarn.

Work 1 row in K.

Change to larger needles, reversed st.st., starting K, and inc. 1 st. each end of every 7th(6th 6th) row to 44(48 52) sts.
Work straight until cream measures 9(9½ 11)in, 23(24 28)cm, or desired length to underarm.
Mark this row.
Work 6(8 9) rows straight.
Cast off loosely.

Neckband
Carefully join both shoulder seams, leaving a 3¾(4¼ 4¼)in, 9½(11 11)cm back neck, using back stitch. With right side facing, using smaller needles and green yarn, pick up and K4(5 5) sts from the holder at the right front neck; 12 sts up the right front slope; 18(20 20) sts across the back neck; 12 sts down the left front slope; 4(5 5) sts from the holder at the left front neck: 50(54 54) sts.
Work 4 rows in green yarn, starting with a P row, and inc. 1 st. at each end of every row: 58(62 62) sts.
Next row: dec. 1 st. at each end of row.

Change to red yarn.
Dec. 1 st. at each end of next 3 rows: 50(54 54) sts.
Cast off loosely.

Front bands
Both alike.
Using smaller needles and green yarn, and with right side facing, pick up evenly down the complete, cream only, edge of the front at the rate of 19 sts per 4in (10cm): 59(62 66) sts.
Work 4 rows in green yarn, starting with a P row, and inc. 1 st. at each end of every row: 67(70 74) sts.
Next row: dec. 1 st. at each end of row.

Change to red yarn.
Dec. 1 st. at each end of next 3 rows: 59(62 66) sts.
Cast off loosely.

Making up
Do not press. Join sleeve seams up to marked point, then insert sleeves, joining rem. of sleeve edges to each side of the base of the armhole and the rem. of the sleeve (i.e. the cast off edge) to the armhole sides.
Join mitred corners of coloured bands in self colours. Catch red edge of bands on to the right side at the first cream row, taking care that they roll evenly. Make a loop buttonhole in red and green used together. Attach button to match.